Making Computers Work for Administrators

Kenneth C. Green, *Editor*
University of California, Los Angeles

Steven W. Gilbert, *Editor*
EDUCOM

NEW DIRECTIONS FOR HIGHER EDUCATION
MARTIN KRAMER, *Editor-in-Chief*
University of California, Berkeley

Number 62, Summer 1988

Paperback sourcebooks in
The Jossey-Bass Higher Education Series

Jossey-Bass Inc., Publishers
San Francisco • London

Kenneth C. Green, Steven W. Gilbert (eds.).
Making Computers Work for Administrators.
New Directions for Higher Education, no. 62.
Volume XVI, number 2.
San Francisco: Jossey-Bass, 1988.

New Directions for Higher Education
Martin Kramer, *Editor-in-Chief*

Copyright © 1988 by Jossey-Bass Inc., Publishers
and
Jossey-Bass Limited

Copyright under International, Pan American, and Universal Copyright Conventions. All rights reserved. No part of this issue may be reproduced in any form—except for brief quotation (not to exceed 500 words) in a review or professional work—without permission in writing from the publishers.

New Directions for Higher Education is published quarterly by Jossey-Bass Inc., Publishers (publication number USPS 990-880). *New Directions* is numbered sequentially—please order extra copies by sequential number. The volume and issue numbers above are included for the convenience of libraries. Second-class postage paid at San Francisco, California, and at additional mailing offices. POSTMASTER: Send address changes to Jossey-Bass Inc., Publishers, 350 Sansome Street, San Francisco, California 94104.

Editorial correspondence should be sent to the Editor-in-Chief, Martin Kramer, 2807 Shasta Road, Berkeley, California 94708.

Library of Congress Catalog Card Number LC 85-644752

International Standard Serial Number ISSN 0271-0560

International Standard Book Number ISBN 1-55542-919-X

Cover art by WILLI BAUM

Manufactured in the United States of America. Printed on acid-free paper.

Ordering Information

The paperback sourcebooks listed below are published quarterly and can be ordered either by subscription or single copy.

Subscriptions cost $52.00 per year for institutions, agencies, and libraries. Individuals can subscribe at the special rate of $39.00 per year *if payment is by personal check.* (Note that the full rate of $52.00 applies if payment is by institutional check, even if the subscription is designated for an individual.) Standing orders are accepted.

Single copies are available at $12.95 when payment accompanies order. (California, New Jersey, New York, and Washington, D.C., residents please include appropriate sales tax.) For billed orders, cost per copy is $12.95 plus postage and handling.

Substantial discounts are offered to organizations and individuals wishing to purchase bulk quantities of Jossey-Bass sourcebooks. Please inquire.

Please note that these prices are for the calendar year 1988 and are subject to change without notice. Also, some titles may be out of print and therefore not available for sale.

To ensure correct and prompt delivery, all orders must give either the *name of an individual* or an *official purchase order number.* Please submit your order as follows:

Subscriptions: specify series and year subscription is to begin.
Single Copies: specify sourcebook code (such as, HE1) and first two words of title.

Mail orders for United States and Possessions, Australia, New Zealand, Canada, Latin America, and Japan to:
Jossey-Bass Inc., Publishers
350 Sansome Street
San Francisco, California 94104

Mail orders for all other parts of the world to:
Jossey-Bass Limited
28 Banner Street
London EC1Y 8QE

New Directions for Higher Education Series
Martin Kramer, *Editor-in-Chief*

HE1 *Facilitating Faculty Development,* Mervin Freedman
HE2 *Strategies for Budgeting,* George Kaludis
HE3 *Services for Students,* Joseph Katz

HE4	*Evaluating Learning and Teaching,* C. Robert Pace
HE5	*Encountering the Unionized University,* Jack H. Schuster
HE6	*Implementing Field Experience Education,* John Duley
HE7	*Avoiding Conflict in Faculty Personnel Practices,* Richard Peairs
HE8	*Improving Statewide Planning,* James L. Wattenbarger, Louis W. Bender
HE9	*Planning the Future of the Undergraduate College,* Donald G. Trites
HE10	*Individualizing Education by Learning Contracts,* Neal R. Berte
HE11	*Meeting Women's New Educational Needs,* Clare Rose
HE12	*Strategies for Significant Survival,* Clifford T. Stewart, Thomas R. Harvey
HE13	*Promoting Consumer Protection for Students,* Joan S. Stark
HE14	*Expanding Recurrent and Nonformal Education,* David Harman
HE15	*A Comprehensive Approach to Institutional Development,* William Bergquist, William Shoemaker
HE16	*Improving Educational Outcomes,* Oscar Lenning
HE17	*Renewing and Evaluating Teaching,* John A. Centra
HE18	*Redefining Service, Research, and Teaching,* Warren Bryan Martin
HE19	*Managing Turbulence and Change,* John D. Millett
HE20	*Increasing Basic Skills by Developmental Studies,* John E. Roueche
HE21	*Marketing Higher Education,* David W. Barton, Jr.
HE22	*Developing and Evaluating Administrative Leadership,* Charles F. Fisher
HE23	*Admitting and Assisting Students After Bakke,* Alexander W. Astin, Bruce Fuller, Kenneth C. Green
HE24	*Institutional Renewal Through the Improvement of Teaching,* Jerry G. Gaff
HE25	*Assuring Access for the Handicapped,* Martha Ross Redden
HE26	*Assessing Financial Health,* Carol Frances, Sharon L. Coldren
HE27	*Building Bridges to the Public,* Louis T. Benezet, Frances W. Magnusson
HE28	*Preparing for the New Decade,* Larry W. Jones, Franz A. Nowotny
HE29	*Educating Learners of All Ages,* Elinor Greenberg, Kathleen M. O'Donnell, William Bergquist
HE30	*Managing Facilities More Effectively,* Harvey H. Kaiser
HE31	*Rethinking College Responsibilities for Values,* Mary Louise McBee
HE32	*Resolving Conflict in Higher Education,* Jane E. McCarthy
HE33	*Professional Ethics in University Administration,* Ronald H. Stein, M. Carlota Baca
HE34	*New Approaches to Energy Conservation,* Sidney G. Tickton
HE35	*Management Science Applications to Academic Administration,* James A. Wilson
HE36	*Academic Leaders as Managers,* Robert H. Atwell, Madeleine F. Green
HE37	*Designing Academic Program Reviews,* Richard F. Wilson
HE38	*Successful Responses to Financial Difficulties,* Carol Frances
HE39	*Priorities for Academic Libraries,* Thomas J. Galvin, Beverly P. Lynch
HE40	*Meeting Student Aid Needs in a Period of Retrenchment,* Martin Kramer
HE41	*Issues in Faculty Personnel Policies,* Jon W. Fuller
HE42	*Management Techniques for Small and Specialized Institutions,* Andrew J. Falender, John C. Merson
HE43	*Meeting the New Demand for Standards,* Jonathan R. Warren
HE44	*The Expanding Role of Telecommunications in Higher Education,* Pamela J. Tate, Marilyn Kressel
HE45	*Women in Higher Education Administration,* Adrian Tinsley, Cynthia Secor, Sheila Kaplan

HE46 *Keeping Graduate Programs Responsive to National Needs,* Michael J. Pelczar, Jr., Lewis C. Solomon
HE47 *Leadership Roles of Chief Academic Officers,* David G. Brown
HE48 *Financial Incentives for Academic Quality,* John Folger
HE49 *Leadership and Institutional Renewal,* Ralph M. Davis
HE50 *Applying Corporate Management Strategies,* Roger J. Flecher
HE51 *Incentive for Faculty Vitality,* Roger G. Baldwin
HE52 *Making the Budget Process Work,* David J. Berg, Gerald M. Skogley
HE53 *Managing College Enrollments,* Don Hossler
HE54 *Institutional Revival: Case Histories,* Douglas W. Steeples
HE55 *Crisis Management in Higher Education,* Hal Hoverland, Pat McInturff, C. E. Tapie Rohm, Jr.
HE56 *Managing Programs for Learning Outside the Classroom,* Patricia Senn Breivik
HE57 *Creating Career Programs in a Liberal Arts Context,* Mary Ann F. Rehnke
HE58 *Financing Higher Education: Strategies After Tax Reform,* Richard E. Anderson, Joel W. Meyerson
HE59 *Student Outcomes Assessment: What Institutions Stand to Gain,* Diane F. Halpern
HE60 *Increasing Retention: Academic and Student Affairs Administrators in Partnership,* Martha McGinty Stodt, William M. Klepper
HE61 *Leaders on Leadership: The College Presidency,* James L. Fisher, Martha W. Tack

Contents

Editors' Notes 1
Kenneth C. Green, Steven W. Gilbert

1. The New Administrative Computing 5
Kenneth C. Green
Dramatic changes in academic computing have altered the way campus administrators conduct business.

2. Administrative and Organizational Issues in Campus Computing 13
Brian L. Hawkins
The microcomputer has brought about a democratization of resources and a new independence from centralized controls.

3. Distributed Computing 27
Jane N. Ryland
Existing and predicated capabilities must be factored into decisions.

4. Using Campus Data for Decisions 35
John A. Dunn, Jr., Robert H. Glover
Decision support systems are necessarily built in a modular, incremental and evolutionary way.

5. A New Role for Deans in Computing 47
Gerald R. Kissler
The decentralization of computing calls for decision making by deans and faculty committees.

6. The Computer as a Presidental Factotum 57
James L. Powell
Use of computers can become an integral part of the administrative style.

7. Office Implementation: A Case Study 65
Louis S. Albert, Theodore J. Marchese
A step-by-step transition to automation led to a smaller staff and higher individual productivity.

8. A Primer on Campus Networks 71
Sylvia Charp, Duffy Hines
Linkages among computers and their users call for an understanding of the concepts of telecommunications.

Further Resources 79

Index 83

Editors' Notes

Few in the campus community have not been affected by the recent changes in computing. Although perhaps references to the "computing revolution" in higher education are boringly overused, there is little doubt that, rich or poor, large or small, public or private, computing on campuses is now qualitatively and quantitatively very different than it was only five or six years ago. Today we see more systems of various shapes, sizes, and capacity; we also have more users, more demands on the data system, and more requests for information.

This volume offers a look at the past and coming changes in computing. The chapters focus on three themes: *personal use,* what can I do with my machine? *office implementation,* how might my office make use of this technology? what issues should we consider as we attempt to acquire and implement new technologies? and *campus policy issues,* what should concern this campus as we address administrative computing needs in the 1980s and beyond?

Chapter One, by Kenneth C. Green, begins with a brief overview of the new computing in higher education, focusing on the recent changes in the personal use of computing and on the personnel who now work with computers. An array of organizational issues affecting campus computing are described in Chapter Two by Brian L. Hawkins, vice-president for computing and information services at Brown University. In Chapter Three, Jane N. Ryland, president of CAUSE, looks at distributed computing, and identifies issues that affect both institutional hardware and data bases in the increasingly decentralized campus computing environment. Chapter Four, by John A. Dunn, Jr., and Robert H. Glover, looks at how decision making by campus administrators is affected by computers on campus.

Chapters Five and Six look at some of the people in campus computing. Gerald R. Kissler, vice-provost for planning and development in the College of Letters and Sciences at UCLA, describes some of the new opportunities and responsibilities for deans and program administrators in the organization and delivery of academic computing. James L. Powell, formerly president of Franklin and Marshall College and now beginning a new presidency at Reed College, draws on his experience as a president and a computer user to project how future campus presidents and other administrators might use the computer as an indispensable personal and professional tool. His observations and future visions speak to the personal uses of computing for professionals in academic administration.

1

Office implementation is addressed in Chapter Seven. Louis S. Albert and Theodore J. Marchese offer a case study of the benefits and consequences of computerization, based on their experience at the American Association for Higher Education. Their insights into the implementation process in a mixed-use office reflect the experiences of many academic and administrative units (and users) over the past five years.

Chapter Eight, by Sylvia Charp, editor-in-chief of *T.H.E.* (Technological Horizons in Education) *Journal,* and Duffy Hines, provides a primer on networking, clearly one of the most important (and complex) issues affecting computer use in administrative organizations and campus environments. Charp offers a clear introduction to an issue that will become increasingly important given the growing concern for linking systems and sharing data.

These are interesting and exciting times in campus computing. We may indeed be on the verge of the long-predicted information revolution in higher education. Whatever happens, we do know that campus computing today is qualitatively very different than it has been, drawing on the talents of new users and the capacity of new machines to provide— we hope—information-based solutions to many of the managerial and financial challenges confronting higher education in the final years of the twentieth century.

Kenneth C. Green
Steven W. Gilbert
Editors

Kenneth C. Green is associate director of UCLA's Higher Education Research Institute and associate director of the American Council on Education–UCLA Cooperative Institutional Research Program.

Steven W. Gilbert is vice-president of EDUCOM.

The past decade has seen dramatic changes in administrative computing—more systems, more applications, a new group of computer users, and new opportunities for computer use in campus administration.

The New Administrative Computing

Kenneth C. Green

The computer has become ubiquitous on college campuses and in campus administration over the past three decades. Although largely limited in the late 1960s and early 1970s to the nation's largest and most affluent institutions, today computer systems on even the smallest campuses manage a vast array of information about students, personnel, and institutional finances. There are few campuses today where the computer, especially the desktop computer, is seen as an administrative luxury. Rather, for a new generation of campus administrators and managers (and their faculty counterparts), the computer is an essential tool and a key campus resource. It generates the information that is the currency of modern academic bureaucracy.

Looking back, the "revolution" was not unanticipated, at least not in some ways. A decade ago observers also spoke of a new revolution in computing, one based on the growing utilization of minicomputer systems (Gwynn, 1979, Baldridge and Tierney, 1979). Gwynn (1979, p. 1) described the minicomputer as the near "ideal [system]: a machine big enough to do the job, inexpensive enough to buy, simple enough to use, flexible enough to grow, and available when needed." The language of that revolution sounds familiar even today: more systems, lower costs, more users, more access to data, better information, and more user control over the systems. "Minis" were hailed by many observers as the reasonably priced resource that would permit many (smaller, less affluent) campuses to develop information systems to replace inefficient paper files. While less expensive than the mainframe systems that dominated computing through the 1960s and most of the 1970s, these systems still required technical personnel to manage the computing function and provided some distance between the users/consumers of information and those who produced information.

Few people in the campus community (or elsewhere) anticipated the movement to freestanding desktop systems that began in the late 1970s and exploded throughout the early and mid 1980s. The movement to desktop systems, coupled with the rapid expansion of application opportunities, processing power, storage options, and memory capacity of such systems, means that a growing number of campus administrators are no longer dependent on mainframe or minicomputers for information. More computers, and more kinds of computers, have concurrently brought computing to a new population of users.

As microcomputers (such as the Apple II+ and Apple III systems and the first models of the IBM PC) began to arrive on college campuses in the late 1970s and early 1980s, their advocates spoke with great passion of a new revolution in campus computing in academic and administrative domains. The desktop-based revolution offered comparatively inexpensive computer access and independence from the large systems. It also brought new applications to new users: word processing, financial models, data-base management, and graphics, applications that were unavailable, expensive, or cumbersome in their large-system implementations. Many campuses experienced the computer wars, tension between the newly enfranchised desktop system users and the old guard of computer system staff and directors, over the use microcomputers and the future direction of campus computing policy (see Chapter Two in this volume).

Major Trends

Looking back, in the past five years we have witnessed three major trends in administrative computing and the new role of desktop computers in the campus computing organization. First, the desktops are becoming increasingly powerful. New products from Apple, IBM, Zenith, HP, Sun, and other vendors offer desktop processing power that begins to approach that of far larger systems. Some of today's desktops resemble the minicomputers of not long ago: They offer large hard disk storage (one hundred or more megabytes), large memory (two to sixteen megabytes of memory), and large processing capacity (one to four or even eight or more MIPS—millions-of-instructions-per-second processing speeds). The desktop system typically found in campus offices today has at least twice as much memory as the standard version of IBM's foundation mainframe products of the mid 1960s. The IBM model 360 had a main memory capacity of 256 kilobytes; most office desktops today are at least 512 kilobytes, and many are over 1 megabyte.

Second, we are enfranchising a new cadre of users, individuals of varying professional and work experiences and educational backgrounds who never thought of themselves as computer users, let alone computer professionals. However, they have become users (sometimes unwillingly, sometimes with passion) who are increasingly sophisticated about applications, that is, what they want the machine to do for them. Moreover, once converted to the new systems, they refuse to give them up. They become believers in the new computing and offer personal testimony about the power and benefits of the new systems.

Third, we are beginning to realize that the future of campus computing resides not with one system but the integration of various systems, desktops, minis, and mainframes. Each kind of system brings unique computing resources to campus computing. The new computing gestalt focuses on systems integration through networking to create a computing capacity that is greater than the sum of the parts. Admittedly, we are in the earliest stages of this movement; the technology is still young. But there is little question that the future direction of computing clearly points toward distributed systems (see Chapter Three in this volume).

New Users, New Tasks

As noted above, the dramatic changes in computer hardware and software during this decade have reached new kinds of computer users. Although not computing professionals by either training or disposition, these individuals are nonetheless competent, sophisticated, and often passionate users. While some may have worked with terminals connected to a campus minicomputer or mainframe, their recent introduction to computing most often has involved desktop systems.

How are people using the desktop computers that have appeared in campus offices in growing numbers in recent years? The underlying theme, of course, is personal and professional productivity. The following foundation applications are familiar to almost everyone by now.

- *Word processing and document preparation.* Academic organizations produce paper. Without question, word processing is the base application in almost all offices. As the systems and software become more powerful and sophisticated, many offices will be drawn to desktop publishing, creating in-house documents (reports, newsletters, manuscripts) previously sent out for typesetting and printing.

- *Financial modeling and management.* Spreadsheets, the original microcomputer application, are powerful tools for posing various "what if" kinds of financial and budgeting questions, the questions of increasing concern to campuses today.
- *Data-base management.* Data bases are no longer limited to one campus computer. Individual program and operational centers can develop their own data bases, often drawing on core information from the campuswide system.
- *Graphics.* Data and schematic graphics, difficult and expensive applications in mainframe and minicomputer environments, are core applications in the world of desktop computing.

To this list of initial applications we can also add electronic mail (across-the-campus or across-the-country), outlining (using products such as "More" and "ThinkTank"), form development, accounting, and desktop publishing, among others. Each application offers new resources and benefits; each builds on previous exposure to and expertise in other applications.

Clearly, campus administrators and managers are not unique in the ways they use these (and other) commercial applications. They, like their peers in other organization environments, turn to the new desktop computing for productivity purposes—to do things faster, wiser, and better, and to make more informed decisions about alternatives and consequences.

Office Implementation: The Introduction of Word Processing

Financial modeling and word processing software helped to move the microcomputer out of the hands of hackers and programmers and into the hands of white-collar and professional workers. Word processing and document preparation are core activities in any campus office. Academic organizations (and their administrative units) generate paper, lots of paper. Consequently, it is not surprising that many offices began their initial forays into desktop computing by purchasing personal computers for document preparation. Between 1982 and 1985, personal computers offered a competitive and very cost-effective alternative to the more expensive, dedicated office word processing systems produced by IBM, EXXON (Vydec), and Wang, among others. Many campus offices found a $4,000–$6,000 personal computer system to be a far superior and less expensive alternative to dedicated word processing systems priced at $11,000–$15,000 or more. For example, in 1983, UCLA's Higher Education Research Institute purchased three Apple computers (total cost: $8,500) to replace an $18,000 Vydec word processing system purchased in 1978. The Vydec had been used only by support personnel and only for word processing. In contrast, the Apples were used by professional staff, graduate students, and support staff for word processing, financial modeling, data-base management, and graphics. This same scenario occurred in thousands of campus offices (and in corporate organizations) across the country between 1982 and 1985, and ultimately led to the demise of dedicated word processing systems. The desktop computer offered a less expensive resource capable of multiple applications.

The focus on word processing as a base function creates some interesting cost-benefit models for many campus offices. Word processing alone would justify the cost of a desktop system for most offices. The additional, often untapped, functionality (financial modeling with spreadsheets, schematic and business graphics, data-base management) can, from a cost-benefit perspective, be viewed as marginal as opposed to capital costs. Systems acquired as writing and document preparation resources, often for support staff, assume additional tasks at no significant cost increase (Gilbert and Green, 1986).

New Analytical Resources

Desktop systems and spreadsheets have given rise to a new kind of analytical resource for campus administrators: the modeling template. Whether produced inhouse for use across many departments or created by an outside source to provide standard models and comparative data, the modeling template represents a very useful resource for campus administrators. Inhouse templates can impose order on the budget development and review activities of individual departments; comparisons of unit and categorical costs become easier as these things become more uniform.

Two examples help to identify the usefulness of both models and highlight the differences between them. Many campuses now provide uniform budget templates to individual administrative offices. When completed, these templates are returned to one office. They may be consolidated (through the spreadsheet linking feature of such products as Lotus's "1-2-3," Microsoft's "Excel," Software Associates' "Supercalc 4," or Borland's "Quattro"). In some environments, the spreadsheet data are electronically transferred into the institution's financial data base and can then be run on the mainframe or minicomputer as part of the campus financial management and budgeting activities.

In a slightly different context, many campuses now use comparison templates that allow administrators to view institutional activities (enrollments, expenditures) against the patterns of other colleges. For example, the National Center for Higher Education Management Systems (NCHEMS) in Boulder, Colorado, offers budgetary and enrollment templates based on data from the U.S. Department of Education's Higher Education General Information Survey (HEGIS). Administrators use these spreadsheet templates to compare various types of institutional finances against those of similar institutions. These comparative data help to flag unusual patterns of institutional activity; deviations from sector and subtype patterns can provide early warning of future difficulties.

The New Status of Expertise

One of the most interesting, if often undiscussed, aspects of the new computing is the consequences for office personnel. The range of software applications involved with the desktop systems—initially, spreadsheets for financial modeling and planning and word processing for document preparation—has created increasingly segmented expertise that often is not linked to educational background, professional title, or organizationally defined job tasks. Professional staff may find themselves assisting support staff in certain contexts (financial modeling, data-base design) even as support staff provide technical (or user) support to professional staff. (Similarly, undergraduates often know more about computer systems than the faculty). Thus, the proliferation of computing can lead to new kinds of expertise-based status, a status not defined by traditional roles and titles but rather by knowledge of computing and ability to solve other user's problems.

Summary

The new administrative computing is quite different from its predecessors. It involves different people, who are often engaged in qualitatively different tasks. And it recognizes that one type of computer does not offer a complete solution to the administrative and academic computing needs on college campuses. The changes in administrative computing—those of the past decade and those coming in the next ten years—represent challenging, dynamic, and exciting opportunities for campus administrators interested in harnessing the new technologies for institutional advancement and their own professional development.

References

Baldridge, J. V., and Tierney, M. I. *New Approaches to Management.* San Francisco: Jossey-Bass, 1979.
Gilbert, S. W., and Green, K. C. "The New Computing in Higher Education." *Change,* 1986, *18* (3), 33–50.
Gwynn, J. W. "The New Technology Means Power to the People." In E. M. Staman (ed.), *Examining New Trends in Administrative Computing.* New Directions for Institutional Research, no. 22. San Francisco: Jossey-Bass, 1979.

Kenneth C. Green is associate director of UCLA's Higher Education Research Institute and associate director of the American Council on Education–UCLA Cooperative Institutional Research Program. He has extensive experience training campus administrators and faculty to use microcomputers, is a consulting editor to Academic Computing, *and frequently serves as consultant to computer companies interested in academic and administrative computing in higher education.*

Anticipating the future and making difficult decisions are the only ways most institutions can afford to participate in successive computer revolutions.

Administrative and Organizational Issues in Campus Computing

Brian L. Hawkins

Over the last fifteen years, computing has become one of the hottest topics in academia. The so-called computer revolution on college campuses has created a significant stir in the academic community and is having a definite impact on administrative computing as well. Both academic and administrative computing in the 1980s changed dramatically with the advent of the microcomputer. The microcomputer made computing widely available and reasonably affordable. Many of the important productivity tasks—such as word processing, small data-base activities, and financial analyses using spreadsheets—could now be done more conveniently and independently. The microcomputer has had two important impacts on the campus. The first of these has been a significant change in the democratization of resources; the second has been the ability of both individuals and departments to use technology in a manner that allows a new-found degree of independence from traditional computing structures.

    The history of computing on college campuses has been anything but democratic. The departments with research contracts and grants, or with discretionary monies, essentially created their own computing environments. Since most universities were not prepared to provide the resources that every department might desire, often the growth of computing was done using these "soft" monies. Because the demand for computing from the hard sciences was much greater than that of the humanities and social sciences, the lion's share of resources for computing within the university budget was devoted to these technical areas. The advent of microcomputing on campus has had an egalitarian influence, making information technology fundamentally more available to academic departments that have not traditionally been computer users. There still are disparities in available funding, but the relatively low cost of microcomputers has allowed many departments, especially the humanities, to participate in this information technology.

Another aspect of this democratization is the increased accessibility of computing for undergraduate students. It is only within the last few years that computing has been widely available on most campuses to undergraduate students. When the technology was largely mainframe (or minicomputer) based, a student's exposure to computing was all too likely limited to an introductory programming course, a few SPSS (Statistical Package for the Social Sciences) analyses, and perhaps some specialized senior applications in technical areas. Again, the impact of microcomputing has dramatically enlarged this scope. Many campuses have established clusters of micros that are generally available. Vendors such as Apple and IBM have introduced programs that allow the resale of microcomputers on campus to all faculty, students, and staff, as well as for institutional use. Schools such as the Stevens Institute, Drexel University, Dartmouth, and a host of others began recommending that their students purchase microcomputers as a means of facilitating academic programs and integrating computing applications. Suddenly, computing was something that universities were actively promoting. Computing was no longer limited to the elite; it was widespread throughout the university.

The microcomputing revolution also allowed for a new sense of autonomy and independence previously not associated with computing. Traditionally, users were dependent on those who programmed and operated the computing systems. There was reasonably little flexibility in administrative systems for changes, ad hoc reports, and independent analyses. The microcomputer has had a significant impact on this situation. Microcomputers have provided administrators with new and important tools to manage the business of higher education and have done so in a period in which declining enrollments require such analyses. This newfound autonomy comes both from powerful application programs and from interfaces that are easy to use and understand. The dynamic and ever-changing world of governmental requirements, market shifts, and other societal factors demand flexible systems if information is to be used appropriately. This new independence has allowed many groups in the university to achieve the sense of ownership over their information environments that previously had been extremely difficult to achieve.

The recent revolution caused by microcomputers and all of the associated interest in computing has been more than technological change. This technology has altered the way in which business is conducted in the university and the way in which faculty instruct, but more important, it has had an impact on the social structure of the institution. The impact of this democratization and new-found autonomy is yet to be fully understood, but vast numbers of the university community are now actively involved in the use of information technology. Members of the community are seriously reevaluating the work they do, how they do it, and the way in which they use this new technology. This ever-increasing interest in and access to computing, however, also brings escalating costs and the need to provide new and different services on campus. The issue of how these efforts should be organized and supported requires serious discussion.

Current Organizational Issues

The increased presence and importance of computers on campus has not just affected the manner in which universities conduct their work, it has also made them examine the administrative structures associated with computing. Owing to the increasing complexity, pervasiveness, and financial impact of computing, more and more universities are questioning whether or not the traditional structures are adequate to manage these important resources. There are several important issues to be addressed, including (1) the desirability of having a single computing organization (as opposed to separate academic and administrative units) and the corresponding issue of determining the appropriate reporting relationship for computing, (2) the desirability of creating the position of a chief information officer, and (3) the scope of functional activities that should report through the computing services structure.

Structural Considerations

In the early history of computing, a single computer center often served academic and administrative needs of the university. In the late 1960s and 1970s, a significant number of schools split these responsibilities into two separate entities. The reasons for this division included usage of different system software, different user orientation, and a perceived need for greater autonomy for academic applications, among others. This pattern often necessitated separate mainframe computers, separate staffs, and different user services. With the advent of microcomputing and the associated increase of interest in computing, there has been a movement to reunite all computing under one organizational structure. The decision to reintegrate computing on campus stems from a need for coordination and control and from potential savings due to economies of scale.

Because of concern about the rapid increase of computing-related costs, many administrators have expressed the desire to have a single focal point of responsibility. Further, this integration comes from the recognition that this resource needs serious management attention, and that it cannot be merely administered as a physical resource.

It is not clear whether a unified or divided structure is preferable. Much of the success of either approach depends on the personalities and structures that are specific to a particular campus. Regardless of the preferred structure, it is clear that if a unified structure is not adopted, there must be an increasing degree of coordination among these groups. The rate of change is too fast, the issues too complex, and the costs too high to not have a commonality of purpose and direction. The method of attaining this commonality is irrelevant if the objective is achieved.

If one assumes that there is a unified structure, one must next ask to whom the administrator of computing reports. There are three options: the president, the vice-president for business, or the chief academic officer. Reporting to the president is probably a mistake, as the technical issues and the implications of daily operations are not appropriate to the presidential area of expertise. Furthermore, issues of consistency with academic and administrative missions may well be overlooked. If teaching and research are the primary objectives of the university, then computing should be integrated with the organizational structure dealing with academic affairs. Having computing report through academic affairs, however, is not a solution. The two distinct, and often competing, functions of academic and administrative computing must have the highest degree of cooperation and joint planning, since differences in needs and constituencies compete for finite resources. The head of computing, regardless of title, has two masters to serve. There is legitimate concern on both the academic and administrative sides as to whether the vested interests of each will be served if the computing head reports to the opposite area. The solution is probably not found simply in reporting structure, since the only unified approach would be to have computing report directly to the president of the institution. The key lies in having a high degree of coordination, communication, and joint planning among all parties.

The Chief Information Officer

The integration of administrative and academic computing, in conjunction with the vastly increased scope of information technology on campus, has caused a number of universities to create a senior position: the chief information officer (CIO) who can also be a vice-president or vice-provost (giving rise to the term *computer czar*). The concept of a computer czar has been written about and discussed, far more than it has been implemented (see Baron, 1985; Fleit, 1986). For a number of schools, especially those with heavy commitments to computing, this position has proved to be an important appointment.

When considering the potential role to be played by a chief information officer, one should look at the objectives for such a position and the skills needed by such a person. This position is probably quite different from the technocrat of the 1960s or 1970s who headed computing on campus. The CIO may well be more of a manager and a change agent than the technological leader of the campus. The demands of such a position call for someone who has a solid understanding of the academic culture, good interpersonal skills, and the positional strength to enact policies that may be unpopular with specific constituencies but that act for the greater good of the university.

These attributes suggest that the position requires a persuasive ability and a credibility more likely to come from within the university than from a person imported from another institution. Furthermore, positional strength may be as much a function of key constituencies' confidence in the person as of the power or title held by the individual. Most computer czars of leading schools in computing were faculty members within the institution whose interest in using computers led them to their position as CIO. The diversity of academic backgrounds is also of interest and includes physics, philosophy, biology, political science, history, operations research, computer science, and management. The fact that these individuals were faculty and not staff is significant. Academic credibility on campus may be a necessary, but certainly not a sufficient, condition to adequately meet the demands of the CIO position.

It is necessary to recognize that computing today is big business. The business issues of contracts, cash flow, and cost recovery make it necessary that the CIO also have good administrative and business skills. Because of the scope and complexity of computing today, a significant amount of time needs to be spent on negotiating software licenses, hardware negotiations, and so on. CIOs spend anywhere between 10 and 25 percent of their time off campus in vendor relationship activities. As procedures and practices in this area become more standardized over time, this time commitment should be reduced. Until then, universities must work for acceptable and mutually beneficial precedents in this area.

Approximately fifty schools have now established such a position, the need for which depends on the degree to which computing is central to a given campus. Also, these positions have not yet been fully institutionalized on campus. Often a CIO position is created for a given individual, but when he or she leaves the institution, the position is not always refilled. The increasing role of computing on campus, however, points to a trend toward basing the CIO position on the need to carefully manage this important, yet costly, university resource.

Scope of Responsibility

Information technology is forcing university administrators to examine which specific functions should report to computing. While the solution to these organizational questions will vary from campus to campus, it is important to consider the issues associated with some of these arenas. If all areas in the university dependent on information technology were to report to computing, this would include the entire university. It may be appropriate to consider three different functional areas now being incorporated within computing at some universities. It should be noted that incorporating such areas within computing may lead to greater efficiency and goal attainment but can also create turf battles and institutional conflict.

The first of these areas is telecommunications. With the need for increasing networking of computers and the divestiture of the phone company, both opportunities and dilemmas are presented to the campus. If an institution is considering major capital investment in a phone switch for voice transmission, there must be serious consideration of data transmission needs as well. This is not a simple issue, as there are technological, financial, and administrative questions involved. It is important that the various units involved have close coordination and that there be clearly defined objectives. The fact that both computing and telecommunications use electronic networks does not automatically require a similar organizational structure.

Printing on campus is another area that can be included under computing. With the advent of laser printing, desktop publishing, and computer-to-typesetter capabilities, there is a need for a coordinated campus printing unit. Traditional means of producing hard-copy output must be reexamined within the context of computing and network strategies. The future of print is further confused with changing copying methods, as scanners, digitization of type, and computer-driven laser printing become more affordable solutions. It is certain that the nature of the work in the print shop will change as technology changes. Campuses need to define a coherent method for producing, charging for, and delivering hard-copy output to the community.

The university library is a third area that could be included under information technology. On-line catalogs, electronic circulation systems, and storage of information on optical disks and CD ROMs or electronic libraries, are becoming current practices within the university library.

These technological innovations have caused some administrators to consider merging the computing function with the information services provided by the library. To date, this model of unifying the library and computer center under a single organizational structure has been adopted at very few institutions. There are important considerations related to the academic mission of the university and the library's role within that mission that are central to the decision to unify functions.

When considering incorporation of each of the areas described above, the technological impact that overlaps that function and computing should be appreciated. While there is a need to ensure cooperation and planning among groups, it should not be automatically assumed that the use of technology relegates a given unit to a reporting relationship within computing. These decisions should be based on the merits of furthering institutional mission and goals.

Managing the Computer Revolution

Although the influx of information technology has caused a great deal of excitement on college campuses, it also has placed an ever-increasing burden on administrators trying to find a way to finance this expansion. Historically, the costs of academic and administrative computing accounted for between 2 and 3 percent of the overall university budget. This figure was fairly stable in the 1970s but has soared since about 1984, largely due to the impact of microcomputing, to nearly 5 percent and, for a few technically oriented schools, to over 10 percent. The accounting of exactly what a campus spends on computing is less the issue than is the the recognition that support of computing today requires significant and growing amounts of the university's resources and that the administration and planning of these resources requires considerable direction.

In the late 1960s and 1970s, although there was the need to replace a mainframe computer every few years, the growth and cost increases of campus computing were fairly predictable and linear. With the introduction of microcomputers in the early 1980s, faculty and staff demanded machines and support, but there were no established budgets for these items. Justifications for the expense were that the introduction of microcomputers would reduce mainframe costs and that there would thus be no net increase in computing costs. This hypothesis has yet to be borne out. Instead, any mainframe time that might have been freed up by moving word processing applications to microcomputers was quickly taken up by research and advanced instructional access to the mainframe that was heretofore impossible. Microcomputers do not save computing dollars. Microcomputers may increase individual productivity, slow the rate of mainframe growth, and allow a more cost-effective computing strategy to emerge, but they do not save the campus real dollars. A case can sometimes be made that manual processes would have been incrementally more expensive than computerized systems, but this does not reduce net increases that are real and reflect added cost to the university. The fact that these costs are hypothetically less expensive than the alternative does not make bills any easier to pay.

Computing on campus has become big business. Gone are the days when computing budgets only necessitated salary increases and increases in maintenance contracts for the mainframe operation. Increasingly, budgets for computing are characterized by significant amounts of unallocated or discretionary funds. The explosion of computing on campus has brought on a very real need for planning in the area of campus computing and, specifically, financial planning. What follows are eight principles that are appropriate for the management of information technology in the upcoming years.

1. Develop a Campus Computing Plan. Many campuses have spent considerable time and energy developing comprehensive computing plans. This process not only facilitates a plan for the most effective resource utilization but, more importantly, creates ownership of the direction and justification of the growth of information technology on campus. The document itself may well be far less important than the process of discussion of these issues with all involved constituencies. A campus plan for more than a three- to five-year period is probably inappropriate, as the technology will have changed significantly in such a time frame. Therefore, this rapidly changing rate of technological change must be kept in mind when considering capitalization of equipment and long-term staff commitments.

All too often, computer plans do not take into account obsolescence. Obsolescence implies shorter-term amortization of equipment and financial plans that include funding for replacement and upgrades of existing equipment. While *obsolescence* is the term often used, it has connotations that are too strong. Equipment that is three or four years old is not necessarily useless or inoperative. Admittedly, this older equipment may be slower, have less available software, and occasionally be difficult to repair, but it still can play an important and useful role in campus computing. One university administrator made the astute comment that if "hardware does what you bought it to do, then it is not obsolete." In many ways this is true, and this thought should not be quickly dismissed. Planning for obsolescence must also include migration paths—ways to move on to newer, more powerful systems—for the future abandonment of today's technology. Orderly adoption and disadoption processes must be included in planning.

2. Define the Limits of What Is Supported. All too often computer plans do not pay adequate attention to the related support costs. The capital price of the computer hardware is only a fraction of the total costs involved. These support costs include hardware maintenance, training, software purchase, upgrade costs, network connection costs, consultants, and so forth. Each of these items has its own set of hidden costs as well. For example, if a piece of hardware is difficult to use, more time is necessary for trainers and users to get familiar with the associated software. Where is this "people time" figured into total cost? Some hardware may be inexpensive, but the associated repair costs are high. When a particular brand of computer has twenty-five available word processors, and each requires three days of consultant time for training, how can a campus afford the luxury of allowing everyone to have their own microcomputer? Support costs can range up to five or more times the actual capital cost of the equipment if care is not taken.

Planning issues cannot be implemented if campuses feel obliged to support everything. Limits must be placed on the hardware and software introduced to the campus. Such decisions are difficult and require the involvement of a variety of campus constituencies. Standardization must not be too limiting, nor should it impinge on the individual prerogative of researchers. However, standardization is necessary to guide users; minimize the growth of support personnel; provide quality support in limited areas; increase the cost efficiency of purchases, service, and repair; and allow for orderly migratory paths from obsolete solutions. If a campus is prepared to limit the software and hardware for which it provides central support, there will be a better chance of attaining price breaks, site licenses, and so on. Making difficult decisions may be the only way most campuses can afford to participate in the microcomputing revolution. Some campuses have gone so far as to recommend specific hardware and to include prescribed software with that hardware. Although these efforts toward standardization must be exercised with great caution and within the culture and context of a given institution, they are necessary if computing costs are to be controlled.

3. Develop a Capital Budgeting Process. Since most campuses have a fairly nonexpansive budget (that is, any increase in income is usually offset by inflationary cost increases), the growth of computing must occur at the expense of other university programs or priorities. This zero sum approach to university budgeting is not new, but during periods in which there were more students to pay the bills, the impact was less. In these days of flat growth or even decreases in student enrollment, this problem is exacerbated. The fact that the explosion of information technology has occurred simultaneously with the decline of an available student population (which is expected to continue into the early 1990s) has led to misgivings on many campuses about the relative importance of expenditures on information technology. While early in the 1980s some campuses used this new technology as a way to attract new students, those days are largely gone. In today's environment, it seems that access to computing technology has come to be expected by students and faculty. Given this situation, a number of changes need to take place in the planning for and administration of computing on campus.

With the rate of change presently being experienced and with the capital costs involved, the planning process for computing is seriously constrained if the commitment for computing is not known more than twelve months ahead. The annual budget process used by most universities restricts the kind of planning necessary for computing in today's environment. To put together a multiyear computer plan requires knowledge of resources that can be depended on, and this means a capital budget committed to computing. If a given amount of capital is committed and a plan for all mainframe upgrades, microcomputers, networking, and so on is managed within these parameters, then planning can proceed. If this process is carefully planned and managed, universities can minimize or eliminate those unexpected costs associated with computing that seem to have been so pronounced during the last few years. Certainly, special installations like an all-campus network may be additional, but it is imperative that a coordinated set of plans and committed resources exist if there is to be orderly growth and transition. These costs problems are not going to subside, since the reliance on information technology will most likely increase.

4. Explore Economies of Scale. In order to reduce costs, one must start to examine the concept of economies of scale. On many campuses, there are multiple computer centers. There is an academic center, an administrative computing center, and potentially a host of small departmental centers, each with its own staff, administrative procedures, and overhead. These independent centers were created to allow different organizational units to have the control necessary to accomplish their goals. Recreating all campus central facilities is not the answer, but examining ways in which basic services and support can be combined, while maintaining subunit autonomy, must be explored. This should not be perceived as a retreat to a centralized approach. What is being suggested, is that the potential of networking allows campuses the opportunity to combine the advantages of centralized and distributed computing to an even greater extent. Perhaps the physics department wants its own mainframe for research; the library wants a mainframe dedicated to the on-line catalog system; and the development office wants a mini dedicated for an alumni data base. To accommodate these requirements in the past, three separate rooms would be renovated and separate staffs hired to run each facility to ensure that the departments got full use of the equipment. The issue in the past was control, and physical ownership and location seemed central to this issue. With today's systems and high-speed networks, the physical location of the machines is unrelated to control, since control can be assured by passwords and systems software. It is probably less expensive and more efficient to house a whole group of mainframes in one room, with a single staff supporting the equipment, thereby making more services and depth of services available. Housing a large number of machines and support personnel in a single location may well be more economical to all concerned, without sacrificing access, control, or functionality. This approach may not be appropriate or feasible on all campuses, but the exploration of such economies of scale should be considered.

5. Develop New Income Streams. One way to reduce the net costs of computing is to develop new income streams associated with these new technologies. The practice of having the computer center help pay its own way is certainly not a new concept. Since the 1960s, the sale of time-shared services has been common on many college campuses. Although the demand for these services on traditional mainframes has declined, one can potentially foresee the resurgence of this practice as the demand for supercomputing capabilities increases. Just as was the case in earlier years, such demand is likely to provide income to larger and wealthier campuses and access without enormous capital investment for smaller campuses.

Another income stream can be developed with the sales, service, and repair of microcomputers. The most important role of the resale function is the ability to provide students, faculty, and staff the opportunity to obtain computers at a drastically reduced price. This resale process can be used as part of a campus strategy for computer access, but it also can be used as a means of providing the income to support consultants and other campus services. Although these operations can generate considerable income over the costs of operation, it is imperative that there be conscious decisions made within a campus strategy as to the role of computer resale. This role and the role of service and repair need to be examined in light of departmental and university budgets and within an overall campus strategy before pricing decisions are made.

Use of already existing resources has provided income to a number of campuses. Rental of computer laboratories during slack time periods, training, and continuing education programs have all helped recover some of the campus investment in computing.

6. Carefully Consider Approaches to Student Computing Access. Providing adequate student access to computing is a serious dilemma on campus. Clearly, universities cannot afford to purchase enough machines to meet all student demand. Recognition of this fact caused a number of schools to require their students to have access to a microcomputer. This really is a rather remarkable change in the way in which higher education is financed. When students purchase microcomputers, they are actually helping to capitalize a portion of their own education. They reduce the ongoing costs of the university in that they share in the obsolescence caused by changing technologies. In the long run this will probably keep the costs of higher education down, but in the short run universities need to consider their obligations to their current student communities.

Universities cannot allow information technology to further divide our society between the haves and have nots. Even if it encourages students to purchase microcomputers, the university still has an obligation to provide adequate general, open access to campus-based facilities and thus not penalize those who cannot afford such a purchase. Universities should also consider how they can make the process of student access as easy as possible. A number of universities have developed purchase programs for their students, faculty, and staff that allow these individuals to purchase computers over time. These approaches have been financed through bond issues, through use of endowment income, and so on and have made access available at well below market rates. Admittedly, there are administrative costs associated with such programs, but these need to be weighed against the alternative costs the university might have to face. Recently, a number of computer vendors have also announced programs to facilitate student purchase of microcomputers over time and thus reduce one of the hurdles to providing truly egalitarian access to technology.

7. Define Cost Recovery Plans in Light of the Institutional Mission. One of the most controversial issues in the computing arena is to what degree the university should attempt to recover costs and contain computer usage through a chargeback procedure. Chargeback makes sense in theory, as it creates a system in which the local end users are accountable. The ideal chargeback system is based on several important premises: (1) that there is a rational process for resource allocation; (2) that the demand for computing remains fairly static within groups; (3) that the decisions about allocation are made by informed and appropriate structures within the university and not the computer center; (4) that the allocative procedure encourages full use of computing resources that have been obtained; and (5) that the process does not undermine the payment of fixed resources to which the university has made a commitment. Unfortunately, these premises are seldom, if ever, met in reality. Instead, peculiar accounting systems are developed that may even provide disincentives to the university's basic objectives.

Much has been made of computing and the library model of information availability, that is, that computing be free for everyone to enjoy. The library has never been free. Instead, there was an institutional recognition that this was a critical resource for the university to be supported centrally, and it was determined that payment should not interfere with the basic intellectual life that the library supported. If universities believe these premises about libraries and find that information technology plays an analogous role, then a similar conclusion about chargeback should be drawn. There is a need to minimize individual abuse of the access privilege, but this problem can be dealt with in other ways. If one accepts the premise that information technology is integral to the instructional and research roles of the university, then an effort should be devoted to identifying means in which these objectives can be dealt with in a dynamic manner, with incentives for maximum utilization of existing resources.

8. Share Resources Among Other Universities. With resources as limited as they are on many campuses, there may be new reasons to look for cooperation among nearby colleges and universities. Why should colleges and universities cooperate on information technology when the track record for cooperation among universities on such activities is modest at best? One successful model of cooperation among university libraries is interlibrary loan. Interlibrary loan evolved from scarce resources and a collegial and noncompetitive culture among professional librarians. Those same ingredients appear to be present in the milieu associated with information technology. Just as with libraries, if there is no cooperation, no single group will really have adequate resources.

Already a number of instances of unprecedented cooperation among schools has occurred, ranging from sharing software libraries to drawing on specialized programming expertise at other campuses. This cooperative process provides a greater depth and breadth of support than would be otherwise available. Since we are still very much in the frontier of introducing technology and since the costs are difficult to manage, universities need to make every effort to avoid duplication of effort, develop cooperative strategies, and find new ways to deliver services to their constituencies.

Conclusion

Computing in the university environment is in a state of rapid change, and this situation is not expected to alter in the near future. What is needed are structures and procedures that are flexible and adaptable enough to capture new opportunities while at the same time stable enough to allow a sense of order to each new transition. If universities are to meet these challenges, it will be necessary to involve all parts of the university community, thus building an ownership for the plans that are adopted. Traditional approaches will probably not be adequate to meet the nonlinear types of change associated with information technology. If in fact we are not experiencing *the* computer revolution, but only the most recent in a series of revolutions, then universities need to develop strategies and procedures that allow for major shifts of resources. These strategies demand a new combination of decentralized and centralized participation if the challenges of information technology are to be affordable and manageable in the future.

Although these administrative and managerial efforts will probably involve tremendous effort and significant expense, there are really very few alternatives. The twenty-first century will be the information world that people like Toffler (1980) have described. It will likely be a world in which discussions of computer revolutions will seem ridiculous in light of the commonplace nature of an ever-present technology. To anticipate this future and to attempt to prepare for it is the only alternative. The cost of doing nothing is too great a price to pay.

References

Baron, N. S. "Priesthood and Pedagogy: Examining Presuppositions." *EDUCOM Bulletin*, 1985, *20* (4), 13-16.

Fleit, L. "Choosing a Chief Information Officer—The Myth of the Computer Czar." *AAHE Bulletin*, April 1986, pp. 7-10.

Toffler, A. *The Third Wave.* New York: Avon, 1980.

Brian L. Hawkins is vice-president, computing and information services, at Brown University.

College and university administrators today must deal with both the opportunities and challenges of a bewildering array of alternatives in distributed computing.

Distributed Computing

Jane N. Ryland

In the beginning, there were mainframes. In 1946 the University of Pennsylvania was the first campus to install a general purpose electronic computer, and shortly thereafter the utility of computers for automating administrative record-keeping functions such as fund accounting, admissions, and registration was quickly realized in college and university administration.

At first, predictions of the limited usefulness of the computer deterred manufacturers from recognizing its potential, but the last twenty years have seen an acceleration in the development of computing and information technologies that has speeded our transition from an industrial to an information-based society.

By the early 1970s most of the larger higher education institutions were immersed in systems development and were wrestling with issues of data-base management and the transition from punch card batch processing to on-line systems. As technology advanced, mainframe system capabilities grew exponentially in terms of processing power and data storage capacity. The price of these newly offered systems typically increased slightly, with a significant improvement in the price/performance ratio. These systems were inevitably shared by all the administrative users in the institution and often by researchers and students as well. In the rush to take advantage of economies of scale, institutions entered into joint ventures to share the newest and largest systems, and in some cases, state data processing departments mandated such sharing, not only among state colleges and universities but with other state agencies as well.

About this time, there began to appear on the market several products that spearheaded a major trend in computer development. Some computer manufacturers, rather than offer bigger and more powerful systems, used the advances in technology to develop slower and less powerful systems that were also smaller and much less expensive.

These minicomputers soon found a home on college campuses, often to support student data processing away from the central computer center. Many academic departments found they could acquire a dedicated minicomputer as part of a research grant. This development has resulted in the microcomputer revolution, with smaller and less expensive systems having many times the capability of the early mainframes within reach of virtually every college and university administrator for about the cost of an electric typewriter. Minicomputers have become superminis, and mainframes have become supercomputers; this distributed computing environment presents administrators with the opportunity, and also the dilemma, of choosing the appropriate computing resource for each situation.

The Three-Tiered Systems Environment

The three-tiered distributed computing systems environment is described by Heterick (1986), who argues the importance of determining what campus computing requirements can best be satisfied by global, regional, and personal systems. Such decisions are difficult because they are undeniably influenced by capabilities that exist at the time of the decision and by the best prediction about future capabilities.

Of special interest is the trend to develop new administrative applications to take advantage of distributed computing capabilities. One such application is described by Shumate (1985): A centralized budget system was developed at Duke University to permit the entry and editing of annual budget data by each department using Lotus 1-2-3 on a microcomputer; the transmission of that data to a mainframe for aggregating, refining, and printing; and the production and redistribution of diskettes for departmental use.

Gossett and Neil (1987) describe a facilities management system designed to address problems of data integrity, data responsibility, and data accessibility encountered when transitioning too quickly to fully distributed systems; the system incorporates central storage of data with support for several different administrative areas with diverse equipment and reporting requirements.

Trends

Each year, CAUSE, a professional association for information technology in higher education, collects information from its members regarding administrative information systems using a member-institution profile survey. In December 1986 a monograph was published by CAUSE (Thomas and van Hocsen, 1986) based on several recent surveys. Respondents to the 1985 survey, as reported in this monograph, were asked for the first time to report administrative applications that operate in a distributed processing mode, and the survey results show several applications with a significant percentage of distributed processing designs, including physical plant operations applications and hospital applications.

Data-Base Distribution

Distributed processing suggests the use of computing cycle resources at many locations across the campus, but administrative applications require more than just distributed processing. A more interesting problem concerns the distribution of the data base, or institutional information resource.

The earliest administrative applications were developed in a disjointed fashion, with data files tied closely to the programs for each individual application. Problems with data inconsistency and redundancy argued for an integrated data-base approach and gave rise to a centralized data administration function to deal with information as a valued asset of the institution.

The arrival of distributed processing suggested, however, that some parts of the data base were best maintained locally rather than on the central system; this was accomplished sometimes by design and sometimes by departments simply choosing to maintain redundant files on their minicomputers apart from the central data base. Physical distribution of the data base across several separate systems is relatively straightforward for those at the local processing points who have responsibility for capturing source data into their part of the distributed computer resource and then maintaining and accessing that part of the data base, but it poses considerable difficulty for the user who wants to access parts of the data base stored somewhere else in the distributed system.

Klingenstein and Devine (1985) discuss some of the alternatives for distributed data bases, where the institutional data base is maintained centrally and a soft version is downloaded each night to each campus or noncentral system (that is, a permanent migration of copies of the central data bases and systems to each campus) either all at once or in series.

Connecting the Elements of a Distributed System

We are just reaching a point where various distributed elements of the system are being connected with networking and telecommunications technologies. Without these connections, an administrator might have had on his or her desk a microcomputer, terminals into one or more regional minicomputers, and a terminal into the university mainframe. With these connections, access is facilitated to any part of the data base no matter where it is stored, but so far the broad diversity of the various elements in the distributed system has not been well accommodated.

Heterick (1986) acknowledges the desirability of a "pluralistic" computing environment that allows the inclusion of highly specialized systems yet also recognizes current limitations that require a user to keep track of new resources continually being added in the distributed environment, to know which parts of the data base reside at which locations, and to understand the different protocols for accessing each part of the system. The next step is a standard interface, or single system image, in which the diverse systems and protocols can be commonly described; until this exists, distributed computing cannot be expected to achieve its full potential.

The Myth of Distributed Computing

Conventional wisdom still suggests that the primary institutional information resource is best maintained nonredundantly, whether all together in a central system or distributed across networked systems, and that a distributed computing environment, with global, regional, and personal computing resources is desirable. However, the particular definitions of what is best satisfied at what level is likely due to the systems capabilities that exist at the moment. When our only computers were large and expensive, it was clear that a global system was the only real choice for any computing requirement, since it was impractical for individual administrators or even departments to have their own systems. With the advent of minicomputers, departments could afford their own systems, and it still made sense to share these, but within a more limited circle of users.

Microcomputers, with easy-to-use spreadsheet software and word processing packages, made it practical to acquire personal computing resources. Tasks seem best suited to one or another of the three distributed computing levels, but new technologies are likely to change this and the tendency will be for more and more tasks to be deemed best suited to a level of computing closer to the user and, ultimately, to the personal computing level. Richard Cyert, president of Carnegie-Mellon University (1986, p. 4), states that "a networked system of personal computers can replace time sharing and eliminate many of the problems of time sharing, ... (which) requires a continual purchase of more large computers and terminals" and believes strongly that "the distributed system will become the computer system for all major research universities" (p. 8).

The institutional data base is already being downloaded for use on microcomputers, and this trend will increase as increased band widths permit the faster downloading of larger data-base segments. With new and more powerful processing chips, microcomputers have already been found to provide faster processing in a dedicated mode for some computer-intensive jobs than minicomputers or even mainframes in a time-shared mode. High-quality printing was once a global resource because of the cost of computer peripheral printers; today, many departments are able to easily bear the cost of a laser printer. The maturation of replicated optical disk technology could conceivably permit the regular reproduction of one thousand copies of the entire institutional data base onto an optical disk less than five inches in diameter for access from every administrator's microcomputer! Departmental operational processing might be accomplished in the future on dedicated microcomputers, with the results available via telecommunications to other administrators needing the information. The move to increasingly personal computing resources will be accelerated by the availability of enhanced communications capabilities and interface software that permit appropriate access to the personal computing resources of others within the department and the institution and even outside the institution.

Consequences of Distributed Computing

Administrators are finding that the environment of distributed computing that confronts them today offers opportunities as well as difficulties. When distributed systems reach the point of having a microcomputer on every administrator's desk, productivity is typically significantly enhanced. Charles R. Thomas, former executive director of CAUSE and now a vice-president of Information Associates in Chicago, speaks of a "coefficient of proximity," which means that utilization decreases by 10 percent for every foot your microcomputer is from your desk! However, that promised productivity increase may never be achieved unless an investment in the necessary training is made.

In a distributed environment, the administrator finds a wide variety of tools and services at his or her disposal, including
- Spreadsheets to facilitate numerical calculations, budgeting, and financial projections
- Word processing to greatly ease the task of correspondence and writing reports that comprises so much of the typical administrator's job responsibilities

- Graphics to aid in development of presentations or for inclusion in reports
- Communication linkages to allow electronic contact with colleagues both inside and outside the institution
- Access to information resources in the institutional data base, in specialized segments of the distributed system (such as the library), and in external data-base resources (such as Lockheed's Dialog or Mead Data Central's Lexis and Nexis).

The mainframe-based central computer center is shifting from a resource that supplies computing cycles to an information center that provides training, information, and expertise on the various elements of the distributed system and to a technology integration center that focuses on telecommunications and creates a common interface to diverse systems components. Ewing (1986) suggests that Management Information Systems (MIS) departments will move away from mainframe operations, hardware management, and capacity planning and provide instead telecommunications and very large data-base management, software evaluation and training for users, and management of policies and standards. An important consequence of distributed systems is the increased importance of standards for the protocol and format of communication between system components.

As distributed computing changes the nature of the traditional computer center on campus, it also expands the role of other administrative departments in developing and managing the automation of their own operational processes, whether these be financial record keeping, personnel management, student records, or admissions. This circumstance has led to a recognition of the value of tools such as fourth-generation languages and expert systems with natural language front ends. Only the most rudimentary versions of such tools currently exist, but they will mature and increase significantly in utility in the next decade. Olson (1986) points out that historical salary inequities between computer center staff and other administrative offices can pose a significant political problem as administrative personnel in a distributed computing environment acquire computing skills and demand equity in compensation.

Another consequence is what Keller (1986) calls "a redistribution of power," which inevitably follows the broader distribution of information. As information is more readily available to more individuals in the college or university community, the power associated with that knowledge is transferred from a few to many.

Ownership, Privacy, and Confidentiality of Data

While considerable effort is being expended to provide access to the various parts of a distributed system, parallel efforts are required to prohibit unauthorized access. Staman (1986) makes specific recommendations for establishing policies regarding ownership, confidentiality, privacy, and security of data in light of increased distributed computing. It is important to make these determinations in anticipation of potential conflicts rather than to try to deal with them when a conflict occurs.

References

Cyert, R. M. "The Impact of Microcomputers on Education." *Perspectives in Computing*, 1986, 6 (2), 4-8.
Ewing, T. "The Future of MIS." *InformationWEEK*, December 1, 1986, pp. 26-37.
Gossett, C. L., and Neil, E. N. "Central Data/Decentralized Processing." *CAUSE/EFFECT*, 1987, 10 (1), 26-32.
Heterick, R. C., Jr. "An Information Systems Strategy." *CAUSE/EFFECT*, 1986, 9 (5), 12-19.
Keller, G. "The Brave New World of Higher Education." *CAUSE/EFFECT*, 1986, 9 (5), 3.
Klingenstein, K., and Devine, G. "Distributed Computing: Options in the Eighties." *CAUSE/EFFECT*, 1985, 8 (3), 4-9.
Olson, M. "Against the Tide: Decentralizing Information Resources in a Centralized Environment." *CAUSE/EFFECT*, 1986, 9 (1), 30-34.
Shumate, C. R. "The Best of Both Worlds: An Application Using Micros and the Mainframe." *CAUSE/EFFECT*, 1985, 8 (4), 22-27.
Staman, E. M. "Ownership, Privacy, Confidentiality, and Security of Data." *CAUSE/EFFECT*, 1986, 9 (4), 4-9.
Thomas, C. R., and van Hoesen, D. S. *Administrative Information Systems: The 1985 Profile and Five-Year Trends.* Boulder, Colo.: CAUSE, 1986.

Jane N. Ryland is president of CAUSE, a professional association for computing and information technology in higher education.

Many operational and some tactical informational needs can be well supported with current information technology and campus-based data. But information support for many tactical and most strategic decisions may be aided by multicampus collaboration.

Using Campus Data for Decisions

John A. Dunn, Jr., Robert H. Glover

Types of Decisions and Accompanying Support Systems

The distinction between operational, tactical, and strategic decisions has received much attention in the recent literature, most recently by Cope (1986). Although these three categories are best thought of as areas on a continuum rather than discrete entities, making a distinction between them is useful.

In general, operational decisions tend to be based on detailed, specific, quantitative information; to have a present or immediate-past time orientation; to require a high degree of accuracy; and to be made frequently. The bursar's ability to report on tuition collections at any point in time and on any individual's status is an example of an operational decision. The bursar needs only information from inside the institution and can typically retrieve information quickly and satisfactorily from the institution's own carefully developed management information system.

Tactical decisions tend to be somewhat more complex. They have a present-to-future time orientation, require more aggregated information, introduce qualitative dimensions, and may require information from outside the organization. The chief business officer's selection of a different mix of tuition payment plans can be an example: How many students are now paying through each plan? What will the impact of the change be on cash flow or on the attractiveness of the institution to students and parents? Are any competing institutions offering different plans? These decisions can often be modeled, with results that show optimal ranges of choice. In this case, however, institutional information systems are only beginning to be helpful. Recent developments in the area of decision support systems aid decision makers in gaining practical access to data bases, extracting relevant information, and feeding data into flexible worksheet or other analytical or modeling tools.

At the far end of the spectrum, strategic decisions in a particular area are usually infrequent, imprecise, future oriented, based on impressions (because hard data are unavailable), and shaped by judgment and aspirations. The president's long-term tuition pricing and financial aid strategy is an example: Where does the institution want to be vis-à-vis competing institutions? What best serves the student clientele whose needs the institution strives to meet? What social and economic pressures should be taken into account and to what extent? What is the trade-off between incremental tuition revenues (involving some student hardship) and strengthened programs that benefit the students who do attend? For these decisions, currently available institutional information systems are generally unhelpful. Some executive-level information can be extracted from them, in the form of summary tables or graphs that portray the institution's current status but the decision requires outside as well as inside information for a valid and useful picture of the institution's history, mission, and competitive position, as well as judgment.

These three types of decisions require different information support systems, as discussed in the following sections.

Operational Decisions: Transaction Processing and Operational Reporting. Transaction processing and operational reporting are largely performed on mainframe and minicomputers, where large volumes of transactions are processed efficiently; a centralized on-line, administrative data base is built and maintained through multiple departments and computer terminals; and operational batch reports are printed nightly on high-speed printers. Direct users of on-line administrative application systems are primarily clerical staff members and their immediate supervisors, who enter, validate, and access individual records (for students, courses, funds, faculty, staff, alumni, or accounts). Batch reports are programmed in COBOL, FORTRAN, or BASIC, with predefined reporting options, or a report generator is used to select and sequence records and to prepare listings, labels, tabulations, and special forms.

Development of one's own custom-tailored on-line administrative applications using second- and third-generation programming languages, while efficient in run time and use of computer resources, is extremely labor intensive and costly. Many institutions today purchase administrative application software from outside vendors whose technical expertise and installation experience enables them to bring up operational applications rapidly and to offer on-site training to administrative and clerical staff. Many administrative applications that adequately satisfy user requirements have been developed using the traditional systems life cycle development method. This system starts with a study of the operational, technical, and cost feasibility of the proposed system. The design proceeds from statements of general requirements to detailed specification of each systems component (such as file structures, screens, editing logic, computations, report formats, main logic, and data-base structures). The application then is implemented and refined through the programming, testing, verification, conversion, operational use, maintenance, and enhancement stages. But many problems can arise with this application development method. Users find it very difficult to specify in advance their information requirements with complete accuracy and to understand the complex and voluminous requirements definition document produced by the systems analyst. The time lag from the initial consultation of user and analyst to the development of the requirements document and from the sign-off on specifications to operational implementation frustrates both users and programmers.

Without fourth-generation software productivity tools on the mainframe, the backlog of unsatisfied user requests for computer programming support can only continue to increase pressure on the limited resources of the computer staff. To avoid excessive dependence on outside vendors and to respond to user requests in a more flexible and timely way, computer services staff must be oriented and retrained in the use of such application development tools in a prototyping environment (for example, active and integrated dictionary, screen generator, fourth-generation tools for structured programming, report generator, query language, data base management system (DBMS) support for all file structures and automated documentation).

Tactical Decisions: Decision Support and Institutional Research Systems. Decision support systems (DSS) use fourth-generation software and a prototyping approach, with interactive computing as tools that enable executives and middle managers to access information. Information is targeted for use in strategic planning and management control, where decisions are less structured than are lower-level, operational decisions. A DSS must reflect the way executives and managers think and the conditions under which they have to make decisions. Leadership and decision-making styles vary, and intuition, judgment, and scenarios are often as important as rationality and data access in making critical strategic decisions.

In designing a DSS, experience suggests that the system should satisfy the information requirements of executives, providing the maximum flexibility for converting data into information. However, the menu and screen interfaces to the DSS should be designed for middle managers who occupy key decision support roles within the institution (such as assistant vice-presidents, assistant deans, registrars, directors of the budget, and directors of admissions). Planning and institutional research serves as the information center for designing and building integrated decision support systems and providing whatever education, prototyping, and technical assistance users need to develop their own applications.

The executive information system focuses on the requirements of summary presentation; the decision support system, in contrast, is concerned with the conversion of detailed data into longitudinal or comparative analyses, into models for forecasting, or into aggregate statistical summaries for purposes of analysis.

Decision support systems are necessarily built in a modular, incremental, and evolutionary way, evolving as the information requirements of decision makers change and as fourth-generation application development tools and strategies continue to improve. Based on currently available technology, the most comprehensive and effective strategy for building a DSS combines the best features of mainframe, minicomputer, and microcomputer software with application development methods. The data dictionary, data-base software, and statistical packages are the primary tools for building the DSS, whereas word processing, spreadsheets, graphics, and desktop publishing are the primary tools for designing executive information systems.

A report generator or micro-mainframe link software is used to select records to extract data from the operational data base on the mainframe in a sequence and format that is ready for downloading to the microcomputer or for direct use by statistical analysis packages on the mainframe. At the microcomputer level, a parallel data dictionary is created along with a menu system to import the downloaded data file into the DSS reporting system. The file transfer can be effected from the mainframe directly through the micro-mainframe link, through a local area network and minicomputer or microcomputer used as a file server or through a cache hardware device directly from tape to Bernoulli box.

Although there are a few integrated fourth-generation products available on the market, none is as powerful as interfaced combinations of the best data-base, statistical analysis, spreadsheet, word processing, and graphics packages that are available. The Office of Planning and Institutional Research at the University of Hartford has been successful in implementing a DSS application development strategy that employs this interface approach. DBase III Plus menus and screens, data dictionaries, systems tables, and parameter screens are built to provide a wide range of data processing, decision support, and statistical analysis functions. A few examples illustrate the simplicity and the power of the DSS user interface. The user selects management information system (MIS) reports for execution directly from a report menu by pressing a single key for the code and hitting the enter key. Selection of data files, creation of indexes to sequence records, selection of subsamples, choices of data fields, and the type and format of reports are performed interactively, either separately or in combination. Prior combinations of report parameters can be saved for execution at a later time simply by referring to the use assigned report code. The data base can be split into subfiles or trigger files (that is, record keys only), with as many as seventy subgroups in a single pass of the file based on user-specified record selection statements. Again, using menu selections, data files are imported to the reporting system, and file transfers are employed as necessary to merge data files and letter files for direct mail, to create a SPSS PC data dictionary and use statistical analysis routines on the data base, or to integrate spreadsheets with a customized graphics package. Statistical rollups of financial, enrollment, or faculty data can be performed either on the mainframe or microcomputer from detailed data; the summary data lines can then be used as a data base for performing inquiries at the aggregate level. Computer modeling has been performed directly from the data base, using applications developed in dBase III Plus as well as with the more frequently used summary data approach, using Lotus 1-2-3 as the development tool.

With appropriate fourth-generation software tools, integrated DSS and other reporting applications can be developed interactively through a cyclical process of prototyping that involves dialogue, testing, and refinement between a DSS builder and the user. When effort normally invested in requirements definition is spent on prototyping, several benefits are realized. The user gets immediate feedback and tangible evidence of progress as the data dictionary, menus, screens, and reports are being shaped to information requirements. Also time and effort invested in building the prototype is much less than it would be using traditional system life cycle approaches. Once the feasibility of the prototype has been determined, it can either be refined directly for operational use or used to provide a refined system's definition document and pseudocode for programming an efficient mainframe application. As microcomputers gain speed and file capacity, more and more integrated DSS applications will be developed at this level; compiled versions (Nantucket Clipper) of interpretive data-base software (dBase III) will enable users to process large-volume files more rapidly.

Institutional research systems should be designed to perform the most important analytical studies, using menus and screens to create and modify statistical analysis routines with a minimum of procedural programming. Data-base and statistical analysis routines are currently available and can be interfaced on the mainframe (System 2000 and Statistical Analysis System), the minicomputer (Datatrieve and SPSSx) or the microcomputer level (dBase III Plus and SPSS PC). Integration of data dictionaries can be achieved between data base and statistical analysis software by writing data-base programs that automatically generate the statistical analysis directory from the data-base directory and user specified system tables of variable labels and code descriptions. DSS menu and screen structures can also be written to enable users to construct statistical analysis routines from modules, with options to change report titles, select data files and reporting sequences, select records and data fields, and choose among a range of descriptive or analytical routines to achieve research or reporting objectives. Having saved each part of the analysis requests, the DSS menus and screens are programmed to recombine and execute whatever combination of report modules the user wants to run. At the University of Hartford, this strategy has been used to build integrated institutional research systems for analyzing admissions applicant and prospect data; building a market analysis system for admissions; modeling induced course load matrix data; studying student aid packaging policies; building a student tracking system to study admissions yield, academic performance, and student retention; and analyzing and forecasting faculty salaries.

Institutional researchers are frequently asked to assist in the design, analysis, and interpretation of questionnaire surveys administered to samples of prospective students, enrolled students, faculty, staff, or alumni. When the surveys are administered through national survey research organizations, the value of the information is usually enhanced when it is possible to merge and associate the survey data with operational data. Automated DSS interfaces can easily be programmed to merge the data files and to perform the necessary statistical analysis routines. For locally administered surveys, a DSS for survey research (SAS or SPSS) can be used to create and modify a questionnaire data dictionary, build interactive screens for keying and validating questionnaire data, and produce statistical summaries for selected subsamples, using interactive computing. DSS direct mail applications that merge address data with letter, label, and listing reports provide the necessary support for mailing and follow-up of questionnaires.

Institutional researchers can make more effective use of the technology of word processing and desktop publishing to increase efficiency in preparing research reports and in presenting results to decision makers and to wider audiences. Multiple institutional research reports employing the same analysis often are performed for several colleges, or the same analysis is replicated periodically over time. Word processing offers the advantages of being able to copy common descriptive sections of a report; to insert unique interpretive sections; and (through file transfers, desktop publishing software, or integrated DSS software) to integrate text, tables, and graphics in attractive, executive-summary formats.

Strategic Decisions: Executive Information Systems. An executive information system employs user-friendly menus and screens to enable senior officers to exchange summary information on strategic plans, trends in external and internal indicators, or progress toward key objectives and results. Standards and guidelines are prepared to improve the content and presentation quality of plans and reports. Text, spreadsheets, and graphics are integrated for maximum flexibility in preparing reports for trustees, senior officers, task forces, or wider audiences. The executive information system is built in a distributed environment on personal computers, using (1) desktop publishing software, (2) word-processing software in combination with a file manager and graph-link software, and (3) an integrated software product having text, spreadsheet, and graphics capabilities (Framework of Symphony). Lotus 1-2-3 menus and macros (saved Lotus key strokes) are used to build a report directory that accesses any report from any subdirectory by use of a letter key in combination with the alternate key. Lotus 1-2-3 macros within each spreadsheet are set up to move to each area of the worksheet, to import and export files, to perform computations or forecasts, to bring up graphs, and to print reports. Administrators can learn the techniques for building and integrating templates for the executive information system in a few hours of computer laboratory instruction or in prototyping sessions with an experienced Lotus 1-2-3 user. Until a micro-mainframe link or local area network is installed, the medium of exchange among users is restricted to the Bernoulli box (a portable hard-disk cartridge) or floppy disks.

Collaborative Approaches

There are at least two ways in which institutional collaboration can prove useful: in the sharing of institutional data to facilitate tactical and strategic decisions and in the sharing of information systems development.

Institutional Data Sharing. The idea of formal and informal institutional data sharing is hardly new. Most institutional research or planning offices, and frequently budget managers, academic deans with salary responsibility, and other officials, spend substantial amounts of time trying to collect useful data on how their college or university compares on one dimension or another to a relevant peer or competitor.

There are a wide variety of sources for such information. For several decades, the federal Higher Education General Information Surveys (HEGIS), now redesignated as Integrated Postsecondary Education Data System (IPEDS), has provided basic institutional data on enrollments, faculty, degrees granted, and other matters. Academic and professional organizations regularly organize and carry on specially focused data collections. Among these organizations are the American Association of University Professors (faculty salaries); the College and University Personnel Association (staff and faculty salaries); the National Association of College and University Business Officers (endowment performance); the Council on Financial Aid to Education (CFAE) (voluntary giving); the Association of Physical Plant Administrators (physical plant personnel and costs); and the American Medical Association and other health professions organizations (data on professional programs). A number of consulting companies also provide extensive collections of data.

These sources are basic and extremely valuable. They may, however, present some difficulties. The federal data collections have not recently been available on a timely basis and have had problems of consistency of reporting. Other collections may not include the institutions one is most interested in, may lack pertinent data, or may be expensive. These organizations strive to provide basic data for all relevant institutions, at some sacrifice of detail, timeliness, and analysis.

Most state system offices serve as the collection points for federal data and carry on whatever survey efforts felt to be desirable for state planning activities. These data collections may or may not be useful and available to individual campuses.

To supplement these efforts, a number of consortia have been formed among institutions with similar interests. These are too numerous to list here, but include:

- The Association of American Universities (AAU) Data Exchange, which involves all the public and some of the private university members of the AAU
- The Consortium on Financing Higher Education (CFHE), which includes thirty leading independent national draw colleges and universities
- The Tufts-EDUCOM Data-Sharing Project, which includes thirty-one universities and eighty colleges
- The Urban 13, which is made up of public, urban-based universities
- The Southern University Group of Twenty-Five, which is composed of universities primarily from the Southern Regional Education Board area
- The Multipurpose Interactive Database System (MINDS), which serves 105 Methodist colleges and universities.

These institutional data-sharing activities can be helpful at various decision-making levels. (For greater detail, see Brinkman, 1987.) A prime focus of the AAU Data Exchange is to compare faculty salaries by rank and discipline. Since these universities have to recruit faculty members (an operational decision) and defend their budgets to their respective legislatures (generally, a tactical process), it is particularly useful to have a good grasp on these specific numerical comparisons.

It is for tactical and strategic decisions, however, that comparisons can be most useful. The value of comparisons can best be understood if all concerned realize that the purpose of the comparison is to obtain insight, not data. Any comparison will present problems of comparability of data. No two institutions are truly alike in data definitions or in completeness and accuracy of the data set, much less in such global matters as mission and service area. However, many tactical and most strategic decisions do not depend heavily on precision of data but depend on context, trends, relationships, and values.

Examples may be helpful. At Tufts University, a great deal of effort has gone into fund-raising in the last several years, culminating in the recent successful conclusion of a major capital campaign. Using both national CFAE data and information from the Tufts-EDUCOM Data-Sharing Project institutions, the authors have carefully tracked annual performance on a variety of indicators. At the operational level (for soliciting specific prospects), this information is unhelpful. In budget planning (a tactical process), we have learned that we spend a good deal more per dollar raised than our most successful competitors, and we have found ways to focus expenditures more carefully. But it is clear at the strategic level, that given the magnitude of support and the budget leverage being won by institutions in whose league we wish to play, continued aggressive fund-raising, even at substantial expense, is essential to our future existence.

Several features of this application should be noted. First, what are operational data on gifts or expenses for one institution become, in aggregate, useful for insight when shared with or compared to similar data from other institutions. Second, indicators are much more useful than raw data; examples include the percent of alumni contributing, the ratio of support from individuals to support from organizations, the proportion of support from alumni versus that from unrelated individuals, trends in each of these indicators over time, and the ratio of expenditures or staff personnel to fund-raising results in each area. Third, despite the presence of a fairly comprehensive and extremely helpful national survey, collaboration among a group of similar universities in exchange of additional data that we agreed on collectively was essential to the usefulness of the outcome.

Similarly, specific information on tuition and fee charges for a group of institutions over time provides the possibility of seeing not only one's immediate position in the group (which is tactically important) but also how that position has been changing over time (perhaps providing a basis for strategic decision making). Comparative information on financial aid, again considered over time and in relationship to student charges and admissions trends, can yield insights useful for budget planning and possibly for alternative strategic decisions to focus resources on programs rather than aid.

A further word about the organization may be useful. The Tufts-EDUCOM Data-Sharing Project is a voluntary, dues-supported organization of leading independent colleges and universities whose mission is to support institutional planning and management by facilitating self-assessment and comparisons with peers, using computerized data-handling and analysis techniques. The members exchange data from national or professional surveys as well as group-designed surveys in such areas as student exchanges, admissions, financial aid, and enrollments; libraries, research activities, facilities, personnel, and faculty numbers and compensation; and a broad range of financial data such as operating revenues and expenditures, balance sheets, endowment performance, and voluntary support. The data are reported to all contributors, accompanied by trend indicators, ratios, and comparisons to national data where available, and in constant as well as current dollars. In a number of selected areas, graphs display relative institutional positions or performances. Membership in the group is by consent of the members.

Institutional Information Systems Development. Vendors of hardware, systems software, and application software, as well as a variety of user groups, professional associations, and funded computer projects, offer considerable support to colleges and universities trying to upgrade the effectiveness of their operations through administrative computing. However, support is often lacking on many campuses for administrators who recognize the need to improve their on-campus capacities for strategic planning, decision support, and institutional research.

Since 1984 the New England Regional Computing Program (NER-COMP), a consortium of sixty-four institutions interested in the advancement of computing, has been sponsoring workshops for administrators, institutional researchers, and computer services staff on the application of decision support systems in higher education. Workshops have varied in length from two and one half days to a full week of demonstrations and hands-on application development using IBM PCs (or compatibles), with training offered either to administrative teams on campus or regionally in a central campus location.

Demonstrations, exercises, and prototype applications are offered in the workshops by staff of the Office of Planning and Institutional Research at the University of Hartford, who function as information center staff to the workshop participants, sharing software applications from a repertoire that has been built over the past five years. Fourth-generation software that is widely available in higher education is used to create an integrated DSS application development environment (dBase III Plus, Lotus 1-2-3, Multi-Mate Advantage, SPSS PC Plus, Microsoft

Chart, ABC Statistical Package, Graphwriter). The essence of the consortium idea is that with adequate training, experienced administrators can work with experienced planners, institutional researchers, and computer professionals in a prototyping environment to develop DSS applications rapidly and to satisfy the changing information requirements of decision makers in higher education with a minimal investment in custom programming.

NERCOMP plans to develop this idea further by extending its DSS training program to create a consortium for DSS application development and software exchange among its member institutions and by offering fully documented and tested applications for distribution to its members and to wider audiences at nominal costs.

References

Brinkman, P. (ed.). *Conducting Interinstitutional Comparisons.* New Directions for Institutional Research, no. 53. San Francisco: Jossey-Bass, 1987.

Cope, R. G. "Information System Requirements for Strategic Choices." In P. Callan (ed.), *Environmental Scanning for Strategic Leadership.* New Directions for Institutional Research, no. 52. San Francisco, Jossey-Bass, 1986.

John A. Dunn, Jr., is vice-president, planning, at Tufts University.

Robert H. Glover is director, institutional research and planning, University of Hartford.

The new technology entails a need for new support units and decentralized decision making.

A New Role for Deans in Computing

Gerald R. Kissler

The agenda for a recent gathering of deans of Colleges of Letters, Arts, and Sciences at large West Coast universities included sessions on (1) the effect of changing federal policies on university research programs, (2) posttenure review procedures for faculty, (3) the core curriculum/liberal education debate and other efforts to improve undergraduate education, and (4) budget problems associated with reduced state funds and lower proceeds from the endowment. These same issues could also have been the topics of conversation in any region of the country ten or twenty years ago, but there was one other topic on the agenda that was not on the deans' agenda in 1968 or 1979: computing.

Unlike their predecessors, today's deans talked about the impact of computers on their educational programs, commiserated about the growing student demand for computer classes at a time when it is difficult to hire faculty in computer science, and shared concerns about management problems and rising costs. The dean of the University of Washington reported that an average of $250,000 of new computers were arriving in the College of Arts and Sciences each month. This figure excluded equipment acquired through a large gift from IBM and machines purchased by individual faculty and students from the bookstore. The $250,000 figure was composed primarily of departmental purchases with state funds, individual faculty purchases with contract and grant funds, and some small donations of equipment. Department chairs and individual researchers are buying minicomputers, microcomputers, software packages, and special boards and peripherals (printers, scanners) and are paying increasing amounts for maintaining this equipment.

This distributed computing environment is far different from the tightly centralized academic computing environment of ten to twenty years ago. In fact, figures for the University of Washington, Virginia Tech, and the Pennsylvania State University indicate that for every dollar spent on hardware and software by the central academic computing organization, six to eight dollars are spent at distributed sites. The fact that deans, department chairs, and individual researchers are spending their own funds on computers is further testimony to the impact of the new technology on teaching, research, and departmental administration in colleges and universities throughout the United States.

This is an exciting time in higher education (Gilbert and Green, 1986), as new technologies and new educational applications appear at an increasing rate. At the same time, the new technology places a strain on existing organizations, creating a need for new support units and new policies and demanding additional resources for more machines and additional staff (Kissler, 1986b). And, as computing becomes increasingly decentralized, a new role is evolving for deans of schools and colleges.

The Decentralization of Computing

The technological breakthroughs that have resulted in powerful workstations on the desks of faculty, students, and administrators have also produced a decentralization of decision making about computing. The decentralization of computing creates a new set of responsibilities for deans, whose continuing responsibilities for personnel, budget, space, and educational policy have become more complex and time consuming. No longer can deans expect other administrators to make all computing decisions.

Twenty years ago the director of academic computing at most colleges and universities was responsible for a center that provided virtually all of the computing services for faculty and students. These directors probably knew all of the faculty who were using the computer and what they were using it for. There were no computers in departments, with the possible exception of the Departments of Computer Science or Electrical Engineering. Purchasing, staffing, and operational policy decisions were made centrally by the director with little, if any, consultation with the deans.

In the 1970s, technological advances and price reductions resulted in minicomputers that were affordable by research groups in the sciences and engineering. Granting agencies frequently preferred the use of their funds for minicomputer purchases over buying time on the campus mainframe. This caused some tension between principal investigators and directors of academic computing, particularly when these directors were responsible for screening all computer equipment purchases. The deans, however, remained above the fray, having little involvement in these minicomputer purchases and the resultant tensions. The continuing decline in the cost of minicomputers and the advent of powerful microcomputer workstations have changed this situation. Increasingly, deans are requested to allocate their own funds for computer purchases, maintenance costs, and new staff, largely for research and teaching applications but also for administrative uses.

The decentralization of computing makes sense, because decisions should be made by someone who knows the academic programs and understands the computing needs in the departments. It is no longer possible for a director of either academic computing or administrative computing to know the educational programs and understand the computing needs throughout the campus, particularly at a large and complex institution where applications will differ significantly by discipline. However, individuals are not chosen to be deans on the basis of their knowledge about computing. They are chosen to be academic leaders and administrators. Nonetheless, departmental teaching, research, and administrative activities in all schools and colleges are relying increasingly on computers. Therefore, deans are being forced to make important decisions about computing, regardless of their knowledge of the field.

The decentralization of computing means that many deans will become responsible for academic computing centers at their schools and colleges; this will place deans in the same uncomfortable position that presidents and vice-presidents found themselves in twenty years ago. Two factors make matters worse for deans today. First, the technology is changing far more rapidly. If computer professionals find it very difficult to stay abreast of new developments, how can a dean expect to keep informed? Second, there are now far more people using computers for a wider variety of tasks. Twenty years ago there might have been 50 to 150 faculty on the entire campus using one central computer for a few basic applications. Today there are as many or more faculty in any one school or college at a large university using many different kinds of computers for many different purposes. And, there are far more students and staff using computers today.

As we look to the future, it seems clear that there will be a mixture of computing activities at the departmental, school or college, campus-wide and multicampus/national levels. When networks are installed to connect computers throughout the campus, the role of the director of academic computing is likely to shift from that of the central computing decision maker to coordinator of computing at many different sites and manager of certain shared resources. The central campus mainframe will shift from being the primary provider of computing to a fast computational tool that serves a network of distributed machines.

Academic Computing Plans

Technological advances and our traditions of departmental autonomy and academic freedom mean that most of the power, authority, and responsibility for computing will probably reside at the school or college, department, and individual faculty levels. In order to coordinate activities within their schools and colleges, deans will increasingly form faculty computing committees, following the common practice of faculty user committees that oversee the activities of academic service units (such as vivaria, shops). At the University of California, Los Angeles (UCLA) computing committees have been very effective. Each dean has appointed a computing committee composed of faculty representatives from the departments. These committees have been charged with developing an academic computing plan for the school or college, which has focused primarily on research and teaching requirements. These school and college plans have been presented to individuals at the vice-presidential level for technical review, approval for consistency with overall campus guidelines, and funding. The UCLA committees request plans from each of the departments and mold them into an overarching plan. This is a very bottom-up planning process, one that is appropriate to a large university with highly autonomous departments. Other institutions might find it better to have a more centralized process with more decisions made at the vice-presidential level and restrictions passed on to the deans in the form of planning guidelines. In either case, it seems wise to have a formal planning process with considerable responsibility assigned to the deans.

Any proposals from individuals (for instance, to develop new instructional software for a particular course) are reviewed and approved by the department before submission for inclusion in the plan. This not only prevents the expenditure of resources on idiosyncratic instructional projects that are not used by other faculty when they teach the same class, but also provides an important peer assessment of the quality of proposals. The UCLA committees draw on expertise within the departments, talk to colleagues at other universities, and discuss alternatives with technical staff in the academic computing center. The committees frequently spawn subcommittees to address particular issues. For example, the Social Science Computing Committee generated subcommittees on undergraduate instruction in statistics, bibliographic data bases, management of the minicomputer, and development of a proposal for an interdepartmental master's degree program in statistical methods. Each subcommittee was composed primarily of individuals who were not on the parent committee. This was done intentionally to broaden the circle of faculty involved in the project. At its peak, more than fifty faculty members (about 20 percent of the total social science faculty) were involved in the parent committee, a subcommittee, a departmental committee, or a courseware development project. There has not been another interdepartmental project of any kind that has involved so many faculty or been so successful.

Committee activities and software development projects can consume a considerable amount of faculty time, which can have a detrimental effect on academic careers. Therefore, we at UCLA draw committee members primarily from the tenured faculty, even though younger faculty members frequently have some of the most interesting ideas. Also, programming assistance and released time from teaching are provided to faculty who are involved in developing courseware, so that these projects will not interfere with their research. Partial release from teaching for one term is a good investment if it leads to a significant improvement in the quality of a class.

Students in all fields have been affected by the new technology. UCLA, like many colleges and universities, has made arrangements for students to purchase microcomputers at the institution's discounted price. Even though none of our schools and colleges requires students to purchase a microcomputer, sales to students through UCLA's bookstore continue to be about 150 machines per month. Colleges and universities are also creating drop-in microcomputer laboratories. Students come to these laboratories between classes or in the evenings to complete class assignments. Each of UCLA's laboratories has special software for courses offered by that school or college and is staffed by individuals who can help students when they first come to the laboratory and whenever they encounter problems. More important, students are helping other students in these laboratories. Far from depersonalizing education as some have feared, the new technology is helping to humanize the experience (Kissler, 1986a).

New instructional software is being written throughout the nation, and new distribution mechanisms are being developed faster than institutional royalty policies are being revised to accommodate these new forms of intellectual property. Much of the new courseware is very exciting, but very little of it is computer-assisted instruction (CAI of the old programmed instruction type). Most of it either permits students to research by analyzing information extracted from a data base or to ask "what if?" questions by using a computer-based simulation model. Although deans must continue to struggle with limited budgets, the issue of cost effectiveness is no longer very interesting for two important reasons. First, the effectiveness portion of the equation is very hard to measure, due to a variety of methodological problems. We do know, however, that students are spending more time on assignments that use computers and that they like this form of education. Under these conditions, it seems likely that students will learn more, whether or not pretest/posttest measurements indicate significant differences in learning. Second, whether we can prove educational effectiveness or not, faculty are developing new courseware, and deans will surely be pressured to provide drop-in computer laboratories similar to the teaching laboratories that have been used for years for foreign language instruction.

While the general issue of cost effectiveness is no longer very interesting, deans should be aware that there are techniques for developing better courseware (see Allessi and Trollip, 1985). Other institutions would be wise to follow Stanford University's lead in assigning an instructional design professional to work with faculty who are developing new instructional software. Such a person can conserve valuable faculty time and improve the quality of the courseware, and this could be of considerable benefit to the hundreds of students who will be using an instructional package in the future. These instructional design professionals might be associated with a particular school or college or provided centrally by the media center, the library, or a microcomputer support office.

If deans appoint academic computing committees and expect faculty to develop plans, then resources must be allocated to implement these plans. Deans would be wise to provide resource constraints to the faculty committees before they begin to develop academic computing plans. At UCLA the plans have been funded from a variety of sources under the control of several different administrators (funds for instructional equipment, instructional improvement, academic support, instructional computing, and through a gift from IBM). In fact, the costs were so large that the plans could never have been implemented with only the discretionary resources available to one of the deans or vice-presidents. This is the first time that funds from so many different sources have been combined to fund a particular educational project, but then this is the first time that UCLA has ever had plans such as these.

The UCLA process keeps the responsibility with the deans but relieves some of the pressure through the appointment of faculty committees at the school or college level and the central review of each committee's plan. No resources were allocated until the plan was approved. This provided an obvious incentive to the faculty committees. The new resources allocated for the computing plans have been used to acquire hardware and software (mostly for use by students in the instructional laboratories and by faculty who were developing courseware), to release faculty partially from teaching in order to develop instructional software, and to hire professional staff for local support centers in the schools and colleges. These staff provide short courses for faculty and students on both introductory and advanced topics. Professional staff also customize software for use in particular disciplines. The local support centers are also responsible for administering the drop-in laboratories, but student employees rather than professional staff have usually been hired for these facilities, since students frequently know more about the courses and are less expensive than professional staff.

Administrative Computing

Administrative computing has continued to be more centralized than academic computing throughout higher education (Emery, 1984). Most administrative information systems for student records and financial systems have been developed for central administrative offices that provided information to other campus units. Because these systems were developed centrally, academic schools, colleges, and departments were among the last to receive the direct benefits of modern data processing systems designed especially to meet their needs. Interesting counterexamples are the development of a departmental accounting system in the College of Letters and Science at the University of California, Santa Barbara (Winans, 1986) and an advising system for departmental counselors at North Carolina State University. Occasionally science departments, engineering schools, and business schools have developed systems for inventory control or accounting, but until recently administrative computing has been highly centralized. Once again, the new technology is changing this situation.

Departments that acquired microcomputers for word processing have found that these machines will also run spreadsheet and data-base packages that will effectively meet many departmental needs for accounting purposes and record keeping. With the help of a student programmer, a department can have a new system in a relatively short period of time. However, there are several problems with this approach to departmental information system needs. First, this approach, which appears to be quite inexpensive for any one department, is quite expensive for a school or college with many departments because the costs are repeated as each department develops slight variants on the same system. Second, the systems rapidly outgrow the capabilities of the single-user microcomputer workstation. As the department discovers the need for system enhancements, the size of the data base, the amount of memory required for the program, and the number of users who need access to the data base exceed the capabilities of the existing hardware and software. Sales representatives are happy to sell bigger systems, but hardware and software costs can escalate rapidly, and soon the department will need costly professional staff to maintain and operate the system. Third, because each of the departments develop somewhat different systems, the dean will find it more difficult to get comparable information from the departments. Fourth, much of the data required by these departmental systems (a departmental accounting system) already reside in a central data base. Without coordination with central administrative information systems, the department is forced to reenter these data, with a consequent loss of accuracy and timeliness.

For these reasons, deans would be wise to coordinate the development of departmental information systems with the central administrative computing office. When approaching the director of administrative computing, the dean should recognize that the encounter may not be welcome. First, these directors already have a backlog of systems requirements from central administrative offices and vice-presidents. Second, they know that departmental systems require far more time with a greater number of users, many of whom are convinced that their departmental needs are unique. Third, directors know that as more departments gain remote access to central systems, the problems of maintaining individual rights to privacy and the integrity of central data increase significantly. More enlightened directors of administrative computing, however, will recognize the importance of the academic mission and will be supportive of departmental information systems for the greater good of the educational enterprise. Less enlightened but politically astute directors will recognize the trend toward decentralization of many data processing functions and will join in the development of departmental information systems as a means of maintaining some form of control over administrative computing on campus.

Deans would be wise to prioritize departmental administrative systems projects, giving initial preference to those with relatively short development periods, low cost, and high payoff to the departments. Departmental representatives to the systems development project team should be chosen carefully for both their knowledge and constructive attitudes. In some cases it may even be useful to assign a member of the dean's office staff to the systems development project team; this person can serve as a liaison between the departments and the technical staff, provide initial training as the system is implemented in departments, and give ongoing support as the system is modified and run on a production basis.

Most important, the dean should provide basic leadership by clearly stating that departmental information systems development will be coordinated with the central administrative information systems office. Early timing of this announcement is critical, because departments are more likely to resist coordinated development projects if they have already invested heavily in the development of their own systems. For this reason deans who do not act in the near future will find that the window for cooperative departmental information systems development has closed.

Conclusion

The new technology provides an opportunity to improve academic programs, teach and conduct research in ways that were never before possible, and improve the management of schools and colleges through better departmental information systems. It also presents a significant challenge, as institutions of higher education struggle to find new organizational structures, policies, and resources.

As computing is decentralized, new responsibilities will be given to deans of schools and colleges. This new responsibility can be met by appointing faculty committees to develop academic computing plans for teaching and research needs, by assigning departmental staff to administrative information systems project development teams, and by forming new alliances with the directors responsible for academic and administrative computing. These plans and projects within schools and colleges should draw on expertise in the academic and administrative computing organizations as appropriate to the task and to the evolving role of those units within the institution.

References

Allessi, S. M., and Trollip, S. R. *Computer-Based Instruction: Methods and Development.* Englewood Cliffs, N.J.: Prentice Hall, 1985.

Emery, J. C. "Issues in Building an Information Technology Strategy." *EDUCOM Bulletin*, Fall 1984.

Gilbert, S. W., and Green, K. C. "The New Computing in Higher Education." *Change*, 1986, *18* (3), 33–50.

Kissler, G. R. "Using Computers to Enhance Student Involvement in the Learning Process." Paper presented at the Western Education Computing Conference, Irvine, Calif., November 20, 1986a.

Kissler, G. R. "When They Asked You to Be Provost Did They Tell You That Computing Would Be Part of the Job?" Paper presented at the IBM Seminar for Provosts and Vice-Presidents of Academic Affairs, Santa Cruz, Calif., October 1986b.

Winans, G. T. "Resource Allocation and Utilization in Academic Departments: A Case Study." Paper presented at the annual forum of the Association for Institutional Research, Orlando, Fla., June 23, 1986.

Gerald R. Kissler is vice-provost, planning and academic program development, of the College of Letters and Science, University of California, Los Angeles.

This chapter describes the day of a hypothetical president whose intense use of the computer, though unusual today, might not be so tomorrow.

The Computer as Presidential Factotum

James L. Powell

Early Morning. College President Cooper Barkley's use of the computer begins on this typical day even before he leaves for the office. He turns on his home microcomputer, loads the word processing software, and calls up the latest draft (the eighth) of his chapter on the necessity for confidentiality in peer review. The subject is vital and has needed all his care and creativity (as well as the many revisions he has learned he needs for good writing). He makes the corrections jotted down on the last printed copy, polishes up the concluding and most important section, and copies the file to a disk that he will carry to his office. Although Barkley is set up at home to send files over a telephone line into the college computer network, simply dropping the disk into his shirtpocket and transporting it physically to his office disk reader is foolproof.

8:00 A.M. As he enters his office, Barkley sees the comforting glow of the power light for his hard disk drive, a large storage device that permits rapid access to his files and software.

Last night he was awakened by an idea, and knowing from experience that it will nag him until it is down on paper, he turns on the office microcomputer and quickly types a memo using the word processing software. (Thank goodness he took the time a few years ago to teach himself to touch type, otherwise he could never compose at the keyboard, which would slow him down terribly. And how much more encouraging to see those crisp letters on the screen than his scratchy, nearly illegible handwriting.) He pulls one of the printed copies as it emerges from the laser printer. As always he is impressed with how attractive the memo letterhead looks; it is indistinguishable without a microscope from printed stationery.

Using his office computer as an intelligent terminal, Barkley opens the telecommunication program (with its automated log-on facility) and links to the campus mainframe computer. A check of his incoming electronic mail shows a message from the vice-president for business who wants a meeting to discuss next year's tuition increase but who cannot make the next scheduled staff meeting. The message includes a table printed from the vice-president's spreadsheet that shows past and projected enrollment, tuition, and tuition income. Barkley brings up the calendar software program (it resides on a shared hard disk and incorporates the daily schedules of the vice-presidents for the next month) and notes that each of the vice-presidents has another time slot open the following week. He instructs the program to block off that hour on each of the calendars, exits the program, and sends an electronic mail note announcing the time to each person who should be there. He has done in thirty seconds what used to take secretaries many phone calls, and the meeting is set for a time he finds convenient!

On his desk he finds a copy of the latest version of a foundation proposal that should go out today; he takes one last look at it before signing. The desktop publishing software and the laser printer have produced a beautiful proposal, with very sharp graphics, embedded financial tables from a spreadsheet, and a mix of fonts and type sizes that enhance legibility. One of the enrollment figures does not look correct, however, so Barkley queries the college statistical data base that is stored in the mainframe computer: The figure is wrong, and he pencils in the correct one on the draft. Seldom completely satisfied with anyone else's prose, he rewrites the opening paragraph on his computer (using the built-in thesaurus to find a synonym for a word he does not want to use twice), prints it out, and attaches it to the proposal. He carries the revised manuscript to his secretary and asks that it be taken to Development immediately. (His new version of the opening paragraph requires the whole proposal to be retyped and printed; in the old days there would have been no hope of making such last-minute corrections. Either he would not have dared to ask his secretary, or there simply would not have been time. But since word processing requires that only the changes be retyped, and since the computer does all the readjusting, his corrections can be made and a new copy ready quickly.)

9:00 A.M. The president's electronic calendar shows a meeting set for 10:00 A.M. to decide next year's freshman enrollment target. Although the vice-president and the director of admissions will bring in the necessary information and a recommendation, Barkley likes to have a feel for the numbers himself. He loads the spreadsheet software and calls up the large spreadsheet that contains the college's enrollment and financial projections for the next decade. (This spreadsheet, like the calendar program, resides on a hard disk to which all the senior officers are connected through a local area network. Each can call up spreadsheet, but the software security system allows only the vice-president for business to make changes.)

This spreadsheet model was built two years ago and has proved invaluable; constructing it forced Barkley and his colleagues to identify all the important variables, quantify the way in which they are related, and set down their current levels and amounts. They quickly learned where important information was missing or of poor quality and which factors had the most effect on enrollment and budget. Using the model for on-line, "what if" simulations proved especially useful in communicating with trustees.

The large spreadsheet loads rapidly, and although the projected freshman enrollment target is in line with the long range projection, a budget deficit is shown. Barkley suspects, however, that the latest effects of the bullish stock market on the college's endowment have not been added. He makes a note to send the vice-president for business a message asking him to add the latest endowment figures to the model. Barkley's hunch is that they will erase the deficit and produce a small surplus; then the freshman target can be used unchanged.

The president's calendar shows that one of his advisees (having advisees is one way for a president to try to keep in touch with at least a few students) is coming in the next day. The telecommunication program gives him access to the student's academic record on the campus mainframe, and as it loads, he recalls that this young man plans to be a physician. The student's record, however, shows that last semester he made only a C in organic chemistry. Should Barkley suggest that it is time for the student to consider changing fields or encourage him to try even harder in his science courses? Barkley will decide as they talk.

Just as he closes the file, the telephone rings and the president's assistant tells him that the chair of the Board of Trustees is on the line and wants to know how much progress has been made in getting a letter out to a major development prospect. Barkley loads his outlining software, calls up his previously prepared outline of the letter, and goes over it with the chair, who suggests some additions. They agree that the letter will go out that day.

10:00 A.M. As the quiet, but effective, alarm music on his electronic calendar sounds the hour, the director of admissions and her vice-president come in to discuss the freshman target. They quickly inform the president that early decision applicants are running behind the projection. After the vice-president inserts a disk containing the detailed admissions spreadsheet into the president's computer, they gather around the screen and enter the lower early decision figure to reflect their news: It is clear that unless changes occur in some other category, the freshman target will not be met. They modify the percent of regular applicants to admit and place on the wait list, and the spreadsheet's graphing module shows that only a small adjustment will be necessary to achieve the original target. The overall admit ratio and yield projected should be close to those for last year. Barkley remarks to himself on the much greater feeling of understanding he now has, thanks to this spreadsheet, of how all the factors in admissions interact.

After they leave, Barkley remembers that he had intended to ask the director what effect she thought their new search mail piece was having. He calls up the telecommunication program and sends her an electronic message with the question. She is heading off on a trip almost immediately, but since while traveling she uses a portable computer and modem to access the campus electronic mail system, he will have an answer the next day.

His assistant comes in with the revised and freshly printed foundation proposal; he signs it with pleasure.

11:00 A.M. His assistant also reminds him that the Board of Trustees meets in three weeks and that the mailing, which is to include his written report on the state of the college, must go out soon. As usual, Barkley has many ideas but has put off getting them down and organized, and now it is almost too late. He calls up the outlining program and begins to type as fast as thoughts come to him; the list soon fills a page. He looks it over and notes how the items are interrelated; in a few minutes he has created headings and rearranged items under them. He thinks he has not done badly for twenty minutes of work and decides to let the outline settle in his mind before dictating a draft.

Barkley remembers that last summer at a trustee meeting, the chair asked for a report on the size of the administration; he should have asked him when they were speaking whether he wanted the report at the upcoming meeting. Barkley places a call to the chair, but the line is busy. The chair also happens to be a computer user, and the college has provided him with a modem and a password on the campus mainframe computer. Knowing that he checks his electronic mail often, Barkley leaves a message with the question.

While he is using the telecommunications program, Barkley calls the office of the Washington agency with whom he has been working to learn whether the draft of their committee report is ready. It is and he prints out a copy (and has it days sooner than if he had to wait for the mail). While he is at it, he prints out a copy of the agenda of the next meeting of the committee.

Lunch Meeting. The senior officers assemble in the college board room for a brown bag lunch and discussion of how the capital campaign is going. The group first reviews the detailed plan of the campaign, prepared using project management software. The results show each task in the campaign, identifying the most critical as well as who is responsible for each one and how much time and money is expected to be spent on each. This program has proved to be easy to use and an invaluable management tool.

Next, the vice-president for development hands out charts, printed from her spreadsheet program, that show the results of the campaign to date. She turns on the computer that permanently resides in the board room (it is connected to a projector for comfortable viewing), brings up the spreadsheet program, and inserts her disk.

The same spreadsheet program that was used to prepare the results to date is now used to project forward two years to the end of the campaign. Gifts and numbers of donors in each dollar category are shown, and it is apparent that although trustee gifts have exceeded the expected total, gifts and pledges in the $50,000 to $100,000 category are running well behind; unless there is an offsetting increase somewhere, the campaign will fall short. The administrators try various "what if" assumptions and come to the conclusion that the key is to get more activity from the VIP club of physician alumni: If only 10 percent more of them than initially projected were to make the average gift, the problem would be solved. The vice-president for development agrees to contact the volunteer chair of that committee immediately to offer more staff support.

Barkley then thinks to ask the vice-president if a projection, even a rough one, can be made of the effect of the new tax law on the annual fund. The vice-president replies that her annual fund spreadsheet breaks donors down by dollar categories and that she believes it can be used to simulate the effect.

Finally, the president asks each vice-president to hand in his or her agenda for the various board committees. All except one are neatly printed on the laser printer; Barkley offers a gentle reprimand to the recalcitrant handwriter who says that this weekend, without a doubt, he is taking the computer home to master the word processor program.

1:00 P.M. Back in his office, Barkley calls up the outline of the board report on which he had worked that morning, makes a few changes, and uses it to dictate a rough draft to be typed by his secretary into the network word processing software. (This is the sort of document he can successfully begin with a dictated draft rather than taking time to type himself.)

The next job he tackles—the letter to the major donor requested by the board chair—is of the opposite sort: Too critical for dictation, it needs great care and a personal touch to be persuasive. After reviewing information about the donor in the alumni data base, he places his outline in one window of the computer screen and types a draft into another, enabling him to see both at the same time. This donor is being asked for a gift to cover the cost of a major piece of scientific equipment, and Barkley uses one of the special laser printer fonts to show the donor how his name would appear on the plaque. The draft looks good; he prints a copy and sends it off to the vice-president for development for her comments.

2:00 P.M. In going through the morning's mail, Barkley finds a request from a former associate for a letter of recommendation. He finds the last one he did for her on the hard disk, changes the address, deletes one paragraph and adds another that is more appropriate for this particular position, and prints it out. He dictates replies to several other letters.

Earlier in the week he had asked the vice-president for business to provide a report on budget expenditures to date; his assistant now brings it in. To prepare this report, the vice-president downloaded data to his personal computer from the large, all-college budget program that resides on the mainframe and used a data base/spreadsheet program to analyze the data. Most departments are projected to end the year on target, but as usual the journalism department is over budget. Barkley sends the vice-president an electronic mail message to take the usual action.

His assistant brings in a list of calls to be returned; Barkley begins doing so, using the computer's autodialer for frequently called numbers to save time. During the calls, he uses the notetaker software, which operates as an accessory and can be brought up during any other application, to take notes as he talks. When finished, he prints out the notes and takes them to his assistant for automatic follow-up, filing, and so forth.

3:00 P.M. The chapter on tenure on which he worked early that morning is due in the editor's hands in two days, and Barkley simply must get it out. He inserts the disk he carried from home, brings up the latest draft on the computer, and double-checks for misspellings and typographical errors by running it through the spelling checker program: It identifies two mistakes, and he corrects them. In reading over the critical sections one last time, he discovers that he had typed *there* when he meant *their*—a distinction that escaped the spelling checker and many proofreadings. Barkley makes the correction and saves the file. He knows that he could try to send it to the editor by electronic mail, but his recent attempts to send whole files over the wires have not always worked and have not been worth the time spent. That will change someday, but for now he decides to take the safe route by copying the file to a disk and sending the disk by an express mail delivery system; it will arrive in two days easily.

Also in his morning mail he finds a request for a copy of his resumé from an education association. He calls up the one he has stored on the hard disk, adds the chapter he just sent off as "in press," and prints out the resumé on the laser printer. It looks great!

4:00 P.M. The stock market has closed, and Barkley logs onto one of the major commercial information services to check on the two mutual funds in which college employees may invest their pension contribution. Both funds are up significantly over the day before. (These services have also been valuable to Barkley's assistant in making his travel arrangements.)

A nonprofit board on which he sits has been trying to arrange their next meeting, and a call to their electronic mail system produces a message with the date. He enters it on his calendar and sends back the message that he can attend.

After returning a few more calls, he accesses his most recent speech to an alumni club. He must give another soon, but this version still reads well. He updates the information about several of the fall sports teams, adds a footnote rebutting the latest campus rumor, and prints it out in eighteen-point type so that he can read it without using his glasses.

5:00 P.M. The academic dean comes in to discuss with Barkley a proposed new leave program for junior faculty. The dean's faculty flow spreadsheet includes projections of the tenured faculty who will be on leave as well as estimates of the pattern of junior faculty leaves in the proposed new program. Barkley has been cautious about adding a program that would require the hiring of more part-time faculty replacements, but sees that in most cases the junior leaves will be taking place in departments where other leaves also will be occuring, allowing the bundling of replacements and the hiring of full-time faculty in many of those positions. The dean and he agree to propose the junior leave program to the Board.

Barkley shuts off the office computer for the day and gathers the papers and disks that he needs to take home.

Evening. After dinner he reads for a while, listening to music, and then realizes that he had forgotten to enter his latest compact disc purchases into his music collection data base. He does so on his home computer and views the list of his growing collection with pride. (Only collectors would understand that he has records to which he has not yet listened and needs a system to ensure that he does not buy an unwanted duplicate on his next trip to the record store!)

He spends fifteen minutes on the speed-reading software program; it has improved his speed for relatively easy materials dramatically with little loss of comprehension. Buying this program was one of the best investments he has made.

And speaking of investments, interest rates on home mortgage loans have been dropping, and Barkley and his wife have been discussing when it would make sense to refinance. Barkley calls up his mortgage spreadsheet and enters the latest rate quotation from their lender: With these new rates, the refinancing points could be paid off in only two years. He decides to call tomorrow to lock in the rates and begin the refinancing paperwork.

Finally, he bangs out a newsy letter to his daughter, away at college and never available when he calls, though her answering machine always is!

Bedtime. As he lies in bed waiting for sleep, Barkley casts his mind back over the day and all the uses he has made of technology. His work style has changed radically, but are things really any better as a result? Barkley's answer is an emphatic yes! The clarity of his writing is bound to get better now that he can keep editing until he is satisfied. Since spreadsheets allow him to understand interrelationships more thoroughly and to avoid having to rely exclusively on someone else's presentation and interpretation, the quality of his decision making in quantitative areas must also be improved. And surely his productivity has increased as well. With one of those flashes of insight that sometimes come with semisleep, however, President Cooper Barkley realizes that he probably would be using computers and technology even if his productivity and clarity were no better: He just finds it a lot more fun that way! (For a stimulating account of the possible impact of computing on the lives of a faculty member and a student, as well as an administrator, see Spinrad, 1983.)

Reference

Spinrad, R. J. "The Electronic University." *EDUCOM Bulletin,* Fall/Winter 1983, 4.

James L. Powell, formerly president of Franklin and Marshall College, is now president of Reed College.

Computers redefine—in often unanticipated ways—how people work.

Office Implementation: A Case Study

Louis S. Albert, Theodore J. Marchese

In 1982 office automation at the American Association for Higher Education (AAHE) consisted of an office full of typewriters and adding machines. The irony is that the office was then hard at work on its Spring 1983 National Conference, "Colleges Enter the Information Society," highlighting the emerging uses of microcomputing in colleges and universities. At that time, none of us in the office had ever used a microcomputer.

AAHE is a national, individual-membership organization with two related purposes: to advance the quality of American higher education and to improve the effectiveness of its members as teachers, learners, and administrators. The membership of 6,500 includes presidents, provosts, deans, faculty members, foundation executives, government officials, and others interested in the conduct of higher education. AAHE provides information to members via its annual National Conference on Higher Education, the Association's "flagship" event; through publications—*Change* magazine, the *AAHE Bulletin*, plus various papers and monographs; and through special activities, such as audioteleconferences, regional workshops, and conferences on special issues such as assessment.

The thirteen-person staff of the AAHE national office consists of four senior administrators, seven midlevel administrators and aides, an executive secretary, and a receptionist. Work in the office involves writing and editing, producing mass mailings, building data bases, fulfilling publication orders, and maintaining a budget and financial records. Excluding special grants, the general office budget totals about $700,000 a year.

AAHE Enters the Information Age

The 1983 National Conference was the catalyst that prompted AAHE's decision to evaluate how it works and how it could make that work more efficient. From information gained at a National Conference workshop, "Microcomputers for Academic Users," the authors were convinced that we should purchase microcomputers for the AAHE office. We immediately postponed plans to have secretarial and accounting staff begin training for word processing and financial record keeping on a terminal connected to a mainframe (for which we had already committed a rental fee of nearly $900 a month.)

Then we went shopping. We chose the Epson QX-10, then a popular machine touted in the computer press. It was relatively inexpensive (compared, then, to the IBM PC), came with a superb keyboard and screen (which pleased the staff), and was bundled with its own, very easy to use word processor, VALDOCS (which disarmed computer skeptics). Within a year, we had ten QX-10s in the office, plus four in staff homes. The total cost to AAHE for the computers and peripheral hardware came to about $30,000. Depreciated over five years, the operating budget expense totals $6,000 a year.

This was the beginning. What followed was a long and sometimes vexing learning process. Some of us took to the computer immediately; others took a year or more to break old work habits while learning new skills; only one or two resisted the computer completely. But ultimately we all changed. New uses emerged that we had not initially considered. And, as we gained experience, we added additional computers for special functions, as described in the following section.

Word Processing. Prior to 1983, three secretaries (one of them half time) handled the final preparation of all correspondence, including copy for our publications, grant proposals, and special reports. Their work was accomplished on electric typewriters supplemented by a ten-year-old IBM Memorywriter that cost $375 a month to lease.

To our surprise, when we purchased the Epsons, the first heavy users were senior administrators. We quickly found that we could compose and edit more efficiently on a micro. We could take disks home with us and, by exchanging disks, edit and improve one another's work. As we became proficient, we began to teach the secretaries how to use VAL-DOCS. By early 1984 most of our drafts were composed on disk and then given to a secretary for final correction and printing. By 1985, thanks to letter-quality printers and track-feed stationary, the senior administrators began frequently to produce final copies of correspondence themselves.

When the half-time and the full-time secretaries resigned in 1985 to take other positions, the half-time position was never refilled; the other position was converted to an administrative aide position. In addition, we cancelled our lease on the Memorywriter. By eliminating a half-time salary and lease costs, we saved close to $12,000 a year.

Accounting. The Epsons use a CP/M operating system. When we first looked into accounting software in 1983, we were not satisfied with what was available in CP/M and decided to have our financial administrator use a terminal connected to a mainframe (owned by the American Council on Education) on which there was appropriate software. Lease and support costs totalled nearly $900 a month.

We used this setup for a year, but in 1985, unhappy with the costs and the amount of down time we experienced from mainframe problems, we searched again for appropriate software. We settled on Solomon III, an accounting package that is particularly useful for the kinds of books maintained by nonprofit organizations. (We use its accounts payable and general ledger modules.) But Solomon III runs only on IBM-compatible machines; for this standalone function, then, we left the Epson world for a Compaq Deskpro with a built-in thirty megabyte hard disk. With just a short (one week) training program, we converted our records to Solomon III. We found that it did all that the mainframe program did, but without the downtime; shortly thereafter, we terminated the lease and sold the terminal.

Our new financial records system has proven so efficient that our financial administrator has been able to cut back from full time to twenty-five hours a week (and begin part-time graduate work). Savings in salary and lease costs now total nearly $16,000 a year.

Conference Program Development and Registration. Each year we register about 2,000 individuals for our National Conference on Higher Education. Prior to 1984, to put the program together and process the registrations, we hired three temporary employees at a cost of about $12,000 a year. Registration forms were processed by hand, and separate log books were maintained for workshops and other special activities. After the forms were logged in, they were sent to an outside firm for entry into a computer to generate alphabetized lists, registration badges, and acknowledgment messages.

In late 1983 we hired a consultant to write a conference registration program for use on the Epson QX-10s. Using dBase II, we struggled through the 1984 conference registration process. Bugs in the program, our own unfamiliarity with computers, continued reliance on temporary help, and a very fickle external hard disk drive resulted in a less-than-happy first effort. We saved about $4,000 on outside computing costs, but spent that much and more on the consultant, extra staff, and lost time.

For the 1985 and 1986 conferences, we again engaged a consultant; he got the bugs out of the program and convinced us to use floppy disks so that every computer in the office could be commandeered in a pinch. We used less temporary help and came out about $5,000 dollars ahead for those years. In 1986, with the assistance of the thirteen-year-old son of one of the authors, we smoothed out and updated the registration program at minimal cost, and we achieved a savings of about $8,500 compared to our pre-1984 costs.

Membership. Our membership coordinator was the final convert. Until 1985 she processed membership applications and renewals by hand and sent them off to an outside data processing firm for entry and generation of lists, labels, and renewal notices. The contract costs for this outside service were about $12,000 a year.

We considered using inhouse microcomputers for this function, but decided to go a different route after thinking hard about the amount of staff time needed to produce the needed lists, labels, and notices. We opted for a compromise: We would continue to use the outside data processing firm's mainframe but enter membership data directly from a terminal in our office. We still employ the computer firm, with its able staff and high-speed printers, to produce reports, labels, and renewal notices.

This new procedure eliminates several extra steps in the process, including special batching of membership applications and renewals, deliveries to the computer firm (twenty miles away), their data entry, and so on. Our membership secretary now has direct control over the data base and has been able to free up time to attend to other membership-related activities. A renegotiated contract with the computer firm resulted in a savings of about $4,000 a year.

Other Functions. Over the years we have had computers, we have learned to use them in ways we did not initially anticipate. Using dBase II and a program written by the same thirteen-year-old, an administrative aide now enters daily cash receipts on a QX-10. Our financial administrator, using the Peachcalc spreadsheet software that came with the Epsons, develops our annual budget and related projections. She also maintains a number of employee data bases on spreadsheets. One of the senior administrators is a regular telecommunications user exchanging messages daily with colleagues around the country. Our conference coordinator develops and maintains multiple small specialized mailing lists, using Peachtext's List Manager software. And our managing editor has begun to send edited disks directly to the printer, saving time and typesetting costs.

Concluding Observations

Over the past four years, AAHE has accomplished radical changes in the way it does business. The staff is smaller; individual productivity is up. Since F.Y. 1983, a real savings of about $43,000 per year has resulted. We are still learning. We, like our colleagues on campuses, suffer occasional episodes of "technolust," asking questions such as: What if we had IBMs or a clone or a PC AT and were able to use all of that powerful MS-DOC software? Or should we purchase Macs and laser printers and get into desktop publishing? Are we making a mistake by not networking our existing computers?

These questions come and go. We will eventually have to replace our Epsons but, to date, they have been remarkably repair free and easy to use. And, because they are so much a part of the way we work, we do not usually dwell on what we might be missing. Ours has been a very positive experience. We have discovered the following:

1. There is money to be saved in moving from a manual to an automated office environment. And just as important as money saved, significant gains can be achieved in the quality and character of individual work.

2. Computers redefine the way everybody works in ways that may be unanticipated. We have learned to expect the unexpected in terms of new uses for our "aging" machines and software packages.

3. Choosing high-quality equipment from the outset is well worth the investment. Repair bills have been low, and the frustrations associated with malfunctioning equipment have been almost nonexistent. And from the horror stories we occasionally hear, we are very grateful not to be on someone else's mainframe for the bulk of our work.

4. Having an office full of the same machines is a real plus. A minor repair on one machine does not interrupt anyone's ability to work. And with everyone using the same hardware and software, the office as a whole tends to function as a user group. Most of what we learn, we learn from one another.

5. User friendliness counts for a lot. The VALDOCS word processor, to a professional writer, stacks up as medium powered; but in an office situation, it accomplishes 99 percent of what anybody could imagine doing. It is so transparently easy to use that all in the office use it, and new employees require minimal training. (By contrast, a sister association spent twice what we did on high-powered hardware and software; after a year, just two of its fourteen employees, both secretaries sent off for training, were using these machines.)

What AAHE accomplished with the introduction of microcomputers is in no way exemplary or even unusual. Specifics of machinery and use aside, what we report here typifies a process of change common to the American office of the 1980s. For us and countless others, the micro brought a series of changes that represented real gains in productivity.

Louis S. Albert is vice-president at the American Association for Higher Education.

Theodore J. Marchese is vice-president at the American Association for Higher Education.

An understanding of basic principles of telecommunications is essential for administrators of colleges and universities.

A Primer on Campus Networks

Sylvia Charp, Duffy Hines

Technology, in particular, the computer, has had a major impact on higher education. With the proliferation of microcomputers and personal workstations, the need for the capability to share resources and information became apparent. As the dependence on information accelerated and use of a variety of communication devices increased, information was created, managed, and exchanged by combining computing and communication techniques and facilities. An understanding of the fundamental operational concepts of telecommunications is necessary to better apply technology and more efficiently plan for future growth.

What Are Telecommunications?

In the early 1960s when computers first became of operational value, their use was restricted primarily to essential business and scientific applications. Input and output devices, such as terminals and printers, were located in close proximity to the computer. Soon, physical limitations became less of a problem, and utilization extended beyond the boundaries of the computer room. Signals generated by the computer were sent and received by a computer or terminal. *Telecommunication* is the term used for this process. Telecommunication, which evolved from telephony, a science created to further the use of telephone communications, can be defined as the electronic process that permits the passing of information from one sender to one or more receivers, with the output being in a usable form (printed copy, fixed moving pictures, optical signals). Telecommunications includes all services, products, media, and methodology used to deliver information, from a simple telephone to sophisticated fiber networks.

Through the use of telecommunications, machines talk to one another. Physical limitations imposed by the electronic connection between terminal devices and computers are extended. Distance is not a limitation, therefore, and information can be shared quickly and easily across a campus or city and throughout the world.

Switching. The communication switch is the nerve center of the network. A circuit switch establishes and maintains a physical connection between two or more physical users on demand. Early switches were mechanical devices that methodically "stepped" through the connection process. Today, switches are controlled by special-purpose computers. With more processing power added to the switches, the network demonstrates more intelligence. The basic functions of the switch have remained the same: to establish and maintain a connection between the originator and its destination.

Switches placed at a private location and not on the telephone premises are called private branch exchanges (PBXs). These are communication switches that can serve an individual organization and provide connection to a telephone company's exchange. They perform the switching functions on the user's premises and are installed when major locations require large concentrations of communication services. The buyer is confronted with a divergent range of decisions, which include wiring plans, signaling, maintenance, and training. Size and type of equipment will determine floor space and environmental conditioning (air, temperature, and humidity) requirements.

It is common to share fixed circuits among multiple users. A switching technique that permits this to occur is known as packet switching. User's traffic is bundled into packets, with each packet coded for identification: sender address, destination address, packet number, and so on. The switch reads the destination address and sends the packet on to the appropriate circuit. In a packet switching network with multiple packet switches, consecutive packets destined for the same receiver are transmitted on the best possible route, determined by the destination address, the amount of traffic, and the performance quality of the available circuits.

The packet switch, which is different from the general purpose circuit switch, establishes a connection for each packet of data only as it is being transmitted. This permits multiple users to share the circuits that interconnect the packet switches. The circuit switch establishes and maintains a fixed connection for the duration of a call. Packet switching can provide faster transmission speeds, fewer errors, and lower cost, as costs for each user are determined by the amount of information carried. A major advantage is that costs of the circuit connections between packet switches and the packet switches themselves are shared by the users of the packet-switched network.

Transmission Method. The communications channel carries information in the form of signals, which are the electrical representation of information, such as speech, data, and pictures.

The telecommunication network was originally constructed for voice or analog signal. A normal voice pattern is a constantly changing wave of energy, changing with tone and volume. The telephone transmitter converts the sound emerging from speech into electrical energy, which varies as to amplitude and frequency.

Different from human speech signals, computer-created signals change in a discrete manner. Only two conditions are required to convey information. The signals are represented by a coded set of binary numbers, either a zero or a one (the binary digits). A digital pulse, or signal electrically represents an instantaneous change of condition. Digital signals can be sent on a digital channel or an analog channel. The technique to enable digital signals to be sent on an analog channel is known as modulation. When a modulated signal is received at the other end of the channel, it must be demodulated in order to be recognized by the data equipment.

Multiplexing. Sharing communication facilities among many users controls cost and increases the number of users on a network. One method of sharing is to divide a communications channel among multiple users. This is called time division multiplexing (TDM). A channel's transmission capacity is divided into time slots, each of which can be assigned to a user. For example, a 9,600 bps (bits per second) channel can be divided into eight 1,200 bps slots. Each time slot is dedicated to a user input/output port on the multiplexer. Another multiplexing technique has been developed that redistributes the communication's channel capacity. A statistical multiplexer (STM) allocates the channel capacity, permitting the aggregate speed of the connected terminals to be in excess of the channel capacity. For example, four 1,200 bps terminals could share one 2,400 bps channel by using STM devices. This requires additional electronics to continuously determine the allocation requirements.

Channels. When signals are generated by a computer, they are changed or modulated before they are sent to a communication channel. In communications, a physical or logical path allowing the transmission of information—the electronic path connecting the data sources as it comes from the computer and a receiver—is called a channel. When the signals—voice, data, or video—are received by a computer or terminal, they are changed back, or demodulated, to their original form. Modulation and demodulation are performed by electronic devices called modems, which provide an electrical connection for the terminal equipment.

Channels are also called circuits, lines, access links, and facilities. They are most often provided through wire or coaxial cable and high-frequency radio beams, such as microwave systems and satellites. One channel per telephone line allows each user to send and receive messages without interfering with other users.

Communications channels are either switched or nonswitched. A switched channel, a two-wire circuit, is one that is fixed at one end to a user and connected at the other end to a communications switch. The channel itself is not switched, rather a communications switch interconnects one fixed channel to another fixed channel. An example of a switched channel is telephone service, where the channel is engineered to allow for simultaneous two-way traffic between the sender and the receiver and where the channel's electronic circuit permits one user to talk at a time. The user either dials a telephone number or commands the data equipment to send a prerecorded number to the communications switch. The numbers received by the switch are instructions that determine the desired connection. Once the interconnection is completed, the data system equipment and software take over. Nonswitched channels are either two-wire or four-wire circuits; are used in voice, data, video, and telemetry applications; and are dedicated to a predetermined set of users. A four-wire circuit is designed to allow one pair of wires for sending information and the other for receiving information, thus physically separating the transmission paths.

A two-wire nonswitched channel may be designed for one-way (simplex) traffic or two-way (duplex) traffic. For most data applications, the channel is designed for duplex operation. The channel's bandwidth (carrying capacity expressed in bps) is divided into two transmission pathways. One pathway is used to receive information. Half duplex permits information to flow in one direction at a time. A two-wire channel is usually referred to as a half duplex circuit, and a four-wire channel is generally known as a full duplex circuit.

Wideband digital circuits are being offered for voice and data applications (known as T-1, DS1, or 1.54 megabit). This service provides a circuit consisting of twenty-four time division multiplexed channels, each operating at 64 K bps. Each of the twenty-four channels can be used individually, or the entire capacity of the T-1 circuit can be used for a single high-speed application. The T-1 circuit is usually installed between multiplexors, with the multiplexing equipment allocating the information flow onto the channels. The multiplexing equipment must adhere to the North American transmission standards for 1.544 M bps service in order to be used for transmitting information on the telecommunications network.

Networking

Networks are the means by which telecommunication services are delivered to users. Their components may consist of telephones, data terminals, switches, communication channels, network protocols, and operating software, all of which function together to establish transmission pathways between components.

Planning a communications network is similar to planning a local and national highway system: Every campus may need to be connected, but every town does not need a super highway. Driveways connect to a street, which in turn, move traffic to cross-town thoroughfares, or county and state highway systems.

Local Area Networks (LANs). As a result of the development of high-speed data communication facilities, hardware and software elements combine to facilitate information and resource sharing. Any device can communicate directly with any other device. A single communications facility carries the traffic for all devices, whether the device is a computer, a printer, or a disk drive, and a network interface connects the devices to the communications facility. Owing to its distance limitations, this network is referred to as an LAN, as it is usually limited to a section of a building, an entire building, or a cluster of buildings. Different configurations, or topologies, have been designated. These are bus, star, tree, and ring. The bus is used to distribute information from one device to another, similar to that of a set of track lights that distributes electricity along a fixed track. In a star wiring topology, all communications devices are connected to a central point, normally a switch. The communications facility in a tree topology branches from the source to each communication devices. This topology can serve a wide geographical area. Ring topology places the communications facility in a continuous path, from an originating path to each of the devices served and back. The ring can be extended from one location to another when each location is a point of high concentration. By using a wire concentrator at such a location, many devices can be connected to the ring. The ring, or high-speed interconnection cable, is usually referred to as a backbone.

LANs can be referred to as baseboard or broadband. The term *baseboard* refers to an information signal that has not been modified, or modulated, from its original form by any process. A baseboard LAN is one in which the information signals traverse the network in their baseboard form and the entire transmission capacity of the medium is used to carry the information signals. Ethernet is one of the most popular baseboard LANs. In a broadband LAN, the transmission capacity of the medium used is electronically divided into several transmission channels, permitting the broadband facility to be used for more than one purpose. It is the transmission capacity of a facility that is referred to as bandwidth. This is measured either in cycles per second or bits per second.

Software is needed to control the LAN components. A set of rules (protocols) controls each station's use of the network to avoid collision and guarantee each station in the network access to the network in its turn. The network software is a factor in defining the number of users that can participate in a local area network and how efficiently networks share resources among users.

When dissimilar networks, such as Ethernet and a packet-switched network, need to communicate, gateways are used. When similar LANs need to be connected, which generally requires less sophisticated capabilities, a bridge is used. The main function of a bridge is to administer message traffic between the LANs.

Emerging Network Stations. Integrated Services Digital Network (ISDN) is a national and international activity for the standardization of digital interfaces and network controls. This totally digital network provides transport of voice, data, and video information using a single pair of wires, structured to create an open network standard according to preestablished protocols. In today's environment, multiple loops or connections are required to permit simultaneous transmission of independent information streams for a single user. For example, two lines are required for a computer interaction and a voice call to occur simultaneously. ISDN electronics creates three information channels on the one-pair connections. Two of these channels are identical and are referred to as B channels. Transmission speed on each of these channels is 64,000 bps. Either of the B channels can be used for transmission of digital voice, data, or video. The third channel, referred to as D channel, provides a signaling path. The transmission speed of the D channel is 16,000 bps and is used to transport instructions, such as when to tell the phone to ring, when to display incoming call identification, and so on. Because of the three channels—two B and one D channel—the ISDN access loop is referred to as 2B + D.

The objective of an ISDN is to provide open access to processors, resources, services, and data bases. The ISDN recommendations include a communications system architecture that defines a layer of services and protocols. Each layer performs specific tasks and requires its own unique protocol to function. This seven-layer architecture is called an open system interconnection model (OSI). The layers are referred to as follows:

1. *Physical layer* provides the electrical connection to the network. It is responsible for transmitting and receiving from the network.
2. *Data link layer* performs the variety of choices, including error recovery, flow control, and sequencing (which terminals are receiving). It is considered the media access control layer.

3. *Network layer* accepts outgoing messages and combines messages or segments into packets, adding a header that includes routing information. The routing information used to ensure the packet is sent to the proper destination.
4. *Transport layer* is concerned with message integrity between the source and its destination. Its two other functions are segmenting/reassembling and flow control. Segmenting is used to break up outgoing messages that may be too long for the network to handle efficiently.
5. *Session layer* provides the control functions necessary to establish, manage, and terminate the connections as required to satisfy the user's request.
6. *Presentation layer* accepts the message, logs the message in, and adds a presentation header.
7. *Application layer* logs the message in, interprets the request, and determines what is needed to support the request.

The standard architecture, embedded in the network, will allow all designers of computers, terminals, and PCs to take advantage of the intelligence provided by the protocols. All devices will be capable of interaction with all other devices attached to the network. A standard interface will be provided so that all ISDN devices offered by any vendor can be considered portable and can easily be moved from one location to another in the network, similar to the way standard telephones are moved today.

Advances in Networking. New processes for the handling and transport of information are developing.

Microwave Systems. A microwave system converts voice, data, and video signals to a radio frequency signal, making them suitable for transmission through the air (free space). Microwave systems can be identified through the presence of round, disk-shaped, and horn-shaped antennas mounted on towers and roof tops. The radio frequency signals are beamed from antenna to antenna in a line-of-sight pathway carrying thousands of individual information streams. Newer microwave systems, designed for shorter distances of one to ten miles, are being installed for communications between buildings and across campuses.

Satellites. Satellites are involved in a telecommunications network. These are placed in a stationary orbit above the equator and serve as a relay point between earth stations, which beam the signals to the satellite on a high-frequency beam. The satellite sends the traffic back to earth, covering a wide geographic area on its beam. This technology works well for voice and video traffic. Due to the length of time it takes for a message to be sent and an answer returned through a satellite system, communications planners usually consider using other technologies for data applications.

Fiber Optics. In fiber optic systems, electronic representations are changed to light signals. These fiber optic systems are used to supplement existing wire cable systems, relieving the congestion found in buildings, on campuses, and in metropolitan networks. A cable of fiber optic strands, about the diameter of a pencil, can carry millions of bits of information as compared to the carrying capacity of a wire cable, which is about the diameter of a baseball and consists of hundreds of wire pairs. Dispersed local area networks can be linked together through a combination of fiber optic facilities, with gateways providing access to the world, and enable economical video transmission for conferences, seminars, and educational programs.

Conclusion

Educators are now faced with a great number of decisions regarding vendor selection, equipment compatibility, performance criteria, wire and cable specifications, and installation of selection systems. Fiber optic systems, software layering, and LANs are examples of newly introduced networking trends that have accelerated the convergence of computers and communications.

Where there is a clear distinction between data communications (communication functions) and data processing computer functions, computer control of many functions has been distributed, taken out of the computer, and placed in the network. Intelligent networks are performing such control functions as error checking and automatic routing. Local area networks, metropolitan area networks, and high-capacity (wideband) point-to-point dedicated services provide the means for resource and information sharing.

With the growing need and desire to access information from any data base and the increasing demand for rapid access to information sources, a high-speed network becomes a necessity. Transferring large quantities of information calls for a high-capacity network, a network for all information needs: voice, data, and video.

Sylvia Charp is editor-in-chief of T.H.E. *journal and is a consultant in the use of technology in education and training.*

Duffy Hines is manager, Bell of Pennsylvania.

Further Resources

Professional Associations and Organizations

Various professionals groups in higher education are devoting more and more attention to computing issues. The five groups actively involved in various aspects of campus computing applications are listed below.

AIR (Association for Institutional Research), Florida State University, Tallahassee, Fla.

CAUSE, Boulder, Colo. CAUSE is the organization for people interested in administrative computing.

EDUCOM, Princeton, N.J. EDUCOM serves the community of campus people interested in academic computing.

NACUBO (National Association of College and University Business Officers), Washington, D.C.

NCHEMS (National Center for Higher Education Management Systems), Boulder, Colo.

Reference Materials

New Directions for Institutional Research. Published by Jossey-Bass in cooperation with the Association for Institutional Research (AIR), these quarterly sourcebooks often address various aspects of administrative computing issues, particularly issues involving data utilization for decision making. Selected issues on computing topics are listed below.

Sheehan, B. S. (ed.). *Information Technology: Innovations and Applications.* New Directions for Institutional Research, no. 35. San Francisco: Jossey-Bass, 1982.

Staman, E. M. (ed.). *Examining New Trends in Administrative Computing.* New Directions for Institutional Research, no. 22. San Francisco: Jossey-Bass, 1979.

Tetlow, W. L. (ed.). *Using Microcomputers for Planning and Management Support.* New Directions for Institutional Research, no. 44. San Francisco: Jossey-Bass, 1984.

Additional Resources on Decision-Support Systems

Adamski, L. "Prototyping Is Fast, Effective, Practical; Is Not New, Magical, a Substitute." *Computerworld,* Mar. 6, 1985.
Agin, N. "New Course in DBMS Design." *Computerworld Focus,* Mar. 8, 1985, pp. 33-38.
Glover, R. H. "A Fourth-Generation Approach to Decision Support in a Private University." *CAUSE/EFFECT,* 1985, *8* (2), 25-30.
Kean, P. "A Walk Through Decision Support with Peter Kean." *Computerworld,* Jan. 14, 1985, pp. 10/3-10/16.
Martin, J. *Application Development Without Programmers.* Englewood Cliffs, N.J.: Prentice-Hall, 1982.
Norris, D. M., and Mims, R. S. "A New Maturity for Institutional Planning and Information Management." *Journal of Higher Education,* 1984, *55* (6).
Rohrbaugh, J. "Institutional Research as Decision Support." In J. Rohrbaugh and A. T. McCartt (eds.), *Applying Decision Support Systems in Higher Education.* New Directions for Institutional Research, no. 49. San Francisco: Jossey-Bass, 1986.
Sheehan, B. S. "Measurement for Decision Support." *Research in Higher Education,* 1984, *20,* 193-210.

Recommended Reading About Computing and the Computer Industry

Many academics who have become active (and occasionally avid) computer users have little or no formal background in this area. Listed below are three thoughtful and informative books that offer an introduction to computing and to the history of the computer industry.

Fishman, H. D. *The Computer Establishment.* New York: McGraw Hill, 1981.
Flamm, K. *Creating the Computer: Government, Industry, and High Technology.* Washington, D.C.: Brookings Institution, 1988.

In addition to the titles cited above, campus and commercial bookstores are well stocked with machine- and software-specific reference materials for desktop and microcomputer systems. These are, in general, useful volumes that go beyond product documentation and provide useful information for all users, but especially novices.

Periodicals

Some of the best resources about the ever-changing computer arena are the various periodicals that cover the industry. In the microcomputer and desktop computer arena, these range from specific product-oriented magazines (such as *PC World, PC,* and *MacWorld*) to more industry-oriented publications (*InfoWorld, PC Week, Macintosh Today,* and *MacWeek*), as well as fairly technical publications (for example, *Byte*). All offer valuable and timely information about products and industry trends. Feature-length articles on product issues and industry trends are very informative. Product reviews provide extremely useful information about new hardware and software coming into the market. Some of these publications, for example, *InfoWorld,* and *Macintosh Today,* are controlled-circulation magazines; subscriptions are free to qualified buyers, generally people who have some influence over product purchasing decisions. On occasion, all the periodicals listed above have had feature stories about computing in campus environments.

In the realm of larger systems, *ComputerWorld* and *Datamation* are excellent publications. Oriented toward MIS managers in large corporate environments, these publications nonetheless have much to offer professionals in academic environments.

Although not focused on administrative applications, *Academic Computing,* a controlled-circulation publication begun in 1987, specifically addresses computing in higher education, with an emphasis on curricular and research applications. *Academic Computing* is recommended for anyone in the campus community.

Index

A

ABC Statistical Package, 45
Academic computing: and cost effectiveness, 52; planning committees for, 50-53
Adamski, L., 80
Administrative computing. *See* Computing, administrative
Agin, N., 80
Albert, L. S., 2, 65, 70
Allessi, S. M., 52, 55
American Association for Higher Education (AAHE), 65-70
American Association of University Professors, 42
American Council on Education, 67
American Medical Association, 42
Apple products, 6, 8-9, 14
Association of American Universities (AAU) Data Exchange, 42
Association for Institutional Research (AIR), 79, 80
Association of Physical Plant Administrators, 42

B

Baldridge, J. V., 5, 10
Barkley, C., 57-64
Baron, N. S., 17, 26
Baseboard LAN, 75
Borland products, 9
Brinkman, P., 42, 45
Broadband LAN, 75-76
Budgeting process, for information technology, 21-22

C

California at Los Angeles, University of (UCLA): academic computing plans at, 50-51, 52-53; desktop computing at, 8-9
California at Santa Barbara, University of, administrative computing at, 53
Campus policy issues: dean's role in, 47-55; of distributed computing, 27-33; of information technology, 13-26
CAUSE, 29, 79
Channels, for telecommunication, 73-74
Chargebacks, and institutional mission, 24-25
Charp, S., 2, 71, 78
Chief information officer (CIO), and information technology, 16-18
Coefficient of proximity, and distributed computing, 31
College and University Personnel Association, 42
Compaq products, 67
Computer czar, role of, 17
Computing, administrative: analysis of, 5-12; analytical resources of, 9-10; applications of, 7-8; background on, 5-6; benefits of, 64; dean's role for, 47-55; decentralized, 48-50; for decision making, 35-45; distributed, 27-33; expert users of, 7, 10; information technology issues in, 13-26; office implementation of, 65-70; periodicals on, 11, 12; planning for, 20; and power shifts, 7, 10, 13-14, 32; by president, 57-64; reference materials on, 11; resources on, 10-12; and telecommunications, 71-78; trends in, 6-7
Conference programs, with office implementation, 67-68
Consortia, for data sharing, 42-45
Consortium on Financing Higher Education (CFHE), 42, 43
Cope, R. G., 35, 45
Cost effectiveness: of academic computing, 52; in association offices, 66-68; of information technology, 19-20; for president, 64; of word processing, 9
Council on Financial Aid to Education (CFAE), 42, 43
Cyert, R. M., 30-31, 33

D

Dartmouth College, student computers at, 14
Data-base management: collaborative approaches to, 41-45; for decision making, 35-45; desktop, 8; distributed, 29, 32; and institutional information systems development, 44-45; institutional sharing for, 41-44; presidential use of, 58, 62; and support systems for decision types, 35-41
Datatrieve, 40
dBase products, 38, 39, 40, 44, 67, 68
Deans: and academic computing plans, 50-53; and administrative computing, 53-55; analysis of role for, 47-55; background on, 47-48; conclusion on, 55; and decentralization of computing, 48-50; and departmental information system needs, 53-54
Decision support systems (DSS): application development environment for, 44-45; design of, 37-38; products for, 38-39
Decisions: campus data used for, 35-45; operational, 35, 36-37, 42; strategic, 36, 41, 43, 44; support systems for types of, 35-41; tactical, 35-36, 37-41, 42
Devine, G., 29, 33
Distributive computing: and administrative alternatives, 27-33; background on, 27-28; connecting elements of, 30; consequences of, 31-32; for data-base management of, 29, 32; and deans, 48, 49; myth of, 30-31; and ownership and confidentiality of data, 32-33; in three-tiered systems environment, 28; trends for, 29
Drexel University, student computers at, 14
Duke University, centralized budget system at, 28
Dunn, J. A., Jr., 1, 35, 45

E

Economies of scale, for information technology, 22-23

EDUCOM, 42, 43, 44, 79
Emery, J. C., 53, 55
Epson products, 66-69
Ethernet, 75, 76
Ewing, T., 32, 33
EXXON products, 8

F

Fiber optics, for networks, 78
Financial management and modeling: desktop, 8; and distributed computing, 31; office implementation of, 67, 68; presidential use of, 59, 60, 61, 62, 63-64
Fishman, H. D., 80
Flamm, K., 80
Fleit, L., 17, 26

G

Gilbert, S. W., 2, 9, 10, 48, 55
Glover, R. H., 1, 35, 45, 80
Gossett, C. L., 28, 33
Graphics: desktop, 8; and distributed computing, 32
Graphwriter, 45
Green, K. C., 1, 2, 5, 9, 10, 11, 48, 55
Gwynn, J. W., 5, 10

H

Hartford, University of: decision support system at, 38-39; and information systems development, 44; institutional research system at, 40
Hawkins, B. L., 1, 13, 26
Heterick, R. C., Jr., 28, 30, 33
Hewlett-Packard (HP) computers, 6
Higher Education General Information Survey (HEGIS), 9, 41
Higher Education Research Institute, desktop computing at, 8-9

I

IBM products, 6, 7, 8, 14, 44, 47, 52, 66, 67
Implementation. *See* Office implementation
Income streams, developing, 23
Information technology: and administrative computing issues, 13-26;

chief information officer for, 16-18; conclusion on, 25-26; costs and benefits of, 19-20; and democratization of resources, 13-14; departmental needs for, 53-54; impacts of, 13-15; and independence, 14-15; managing, 19-25; organizational issues of, 15-19; and reporting relationships, 16, 18-19; resource sharing for, 25; responsibility for, 18-19; structural issues of, 15-16

Institutional research: analytical studies by, 39-41; word processing for, 40-41

Instructional software, planning and coordinating, 51-52

Integrated Postsecondary Education Data System (IPEDS), 41

Integrated Services Digital Network (ISDN), 76-77

K

Kean, P., 80
Keller, G., 32, 33
Kissler, G. R., 1, 47, 48, 51, 55
Klingenstein, K., 29, 33

L

Library, and information technology, 18-19, 24-25

Local area network (LAN): for decision support systems, 38; for spreadsheets, 59; in telecommunication, 75-76

Lockheed products, 32
Lotus products, 9, 28, 39, 41, 44

M

Marchese, T. J., 2, 65, 70
Martin, J., 80
Mead Data Central products, 32
Microsoft products, 9, 44-45
Microwave systems, for networks, 77
Mims, R. S., 80
Minicomputers, 5-6, 48-49
Multi-Mate products, 44
Multiplexing, for telecommunication, 73
Multipurpose Interactive Database System (MINDS), 42

N

National Association of College and University Business Officers (NACUBO), 42, 79

National Center for Higher Education Management Systems (NCHEMS), 9, 79

Neil, E. N., 28, 33

Networks: advances in, 77-78; emerging stations for, 76-77; layers of services in, 76-77; local area, 38, 59, 75-76; and telecommunication, 75-78

New England Regional Computing Program (NERCOMP), 44-45

Norris, D. M., 80

North Carolina State University, administrative computing at, 53

O

Obsolescence, planning for, 20

Office implementation: applications in, 66-68; background on, 65-66; case study of, 65-70; and conference programming, 67-68; of financial management and modeling, 67, 68; for membership functions, 68; observations on, 69-70; of telecommunications, 68; and word processing, 8-9, 66-67

Olson, M., 32, 33

Operational decisions: examples of, 35, 42; systems life cycle development method for, 37; transaction processing and operational reporting for, 36-37

P

Packet switching, 72-73
Pennsylvania, University of, first campus mainframe at, 27
Pennsylvania State University, distributed computing at, 48
Personal use, by president, 57-64
Powell, J. L., 1, 57, 64
President, administrative computing by, 57-64
Printing, and information technology, 18
Professional associations, 79

R

Rohrbaugh, J., 80
Ryland, J. N., 1, 27, 33

S

Satellites, for networks, 77
Sheehan, B. S., 79
Shumate, C. R., 28, 33
Software Associates products, 9
Southern Regional Education Board, 42
Southern University Group, 42
Spinrad, R. J., 64
Spreadsheets. *See* Financial management and modeling
Staman, E. M., 33, 79
Stanford University, instructional software at, 52
Statistical Analysis System (SAS), 40
Statistical multiplexer (STM), 73
Statistical Package for the Social Sciences (SPSS), 14, 39, 40, 44
Stevens Institute of Technology, student computers at, 14
Strategic decisions: examples of, 36, 43, 44; executive information systems for, 41
Students: computer ownership by, 14, 51; computing access for, 23-24
Sun computers, 6
Support costs, limits of, 20-21
Switching, in telecommunications, 72-73
System 2000, 40

T

Tactical decisions: examples of, 35-36, 42; support and institutional research systems for, 37-41
Telecommunications: analysis of, 71-78; channels for, 73-74; concept of, 71-72; conclusion on, 78; and distributed computing, 32; elements in, 71-74; and information technology, 18; and networking, 75-78; office implementation of, 68; presidential use of, 58, 59, 60; switching in, 72-73; transmission method for, 73
Templates, in desktop computing, 9-10
Tetlow, W. L., 79
Thomas, C. R., 29, 31, 33
Tierney, M. I., 5, 10
Time division multiplexing (TDM), 73
Toffler, A., 26
Trollip, S. R., 52, 55
Tufts-EDUCOM Data-Sharing Project, 42, 43, 44
Tufts University, fund-raising by, 43

U

U.S. Department of Education, 9
Urban 13, 42
Users, new cadre of, 7, 10

V

van Hoesen, D. S., 29, 33
Virginia Polytechnic Institute and State University, distributed computing at, 48

W

Wang products, 8
Washington, University of, new computers at, 47-48
Winans, G. T., 53, 55
Word processing: cost-benefit model of, 9; desktop, 7; and distributed computing, 31; for institutional research, 40-41; office implementation of, 8-9, 66-67; presidential use of, 57-58, 61, 62-63

Z

Zenith computers, 6